FROM MY JAMAICAN
GULLY TO THE WORLD

DITORIAL
MMITTEE

From L - R: Bevon Barnett, Audrey Wright, (Editor), Sheena Grandis
Anne-Marie Elliott, and Mr. T. Coakley, Staff Adviser.

THE ENVIRONMENTAL JOURNEY OF
AUDREY WRIGHT PETERMAN

My beloved sister Maite! I love you! I love you! I love you endlessly! Love, Audrey #55

SUPPORT FOR *FROM MY JAMAICAN GULLY TO THE WORLD:*

"Audrey Peterman writes like no other about the Jamaica I grew up in. I bet there was a Mass Ding Dong in every parish! Editing her text was a pure delight - I often laughed out loud. I also now have a list of US national parks that I must visit. I'm not into camping, but she also mentions some pretty fine hotels! This book is a splendid gift for our children and grandchildren, in modern Jamaica and especially in the Jamaican diaspora. We applaud and appreciate Audrey's wonderful memory and treasured photographs. A real treat!"

Elaine Douglas-Harrison, Professor

"Audrey Peterman's book is a riveting coming-of-age saga in the era of Michael Manley's Socialist Jamaica. She writes with so much heart and love for our homeland and lays a poignant backdrop for her growth and maturity into an avid advocate of the US parks and public spaces. Audrey's pen is like the brush of an artist and she paints us a picture that evokes memories of Jamaica, Land that We Love. Bravo on this important story!"

Jennifer French-Parker, Publisher, Crossroads News

"Audrey Peterman's passion and work have inspired countless people to connect with the places they love, as well as to protect them for future generations. Her book teaches us that legacy is not what we leave for people, but what we leave in people, and I'm truly grateful to have worked on many efforts with one of the best. One love!"

Robert Hanna, John Muir's great-great-grandson

FOREWORD

My mother says I came into the world in a hurry, August 21, 1951, as if I was on a mission. "All that was missing was your heels and pocketbook," she joked.

I didn't find that mission until my mid-40s, but now I see that my whole life before was preparation. Growing up in Clarendon, Jamaica, spending countless hours sitting on the banks of the gully that ran behind our house; mesmerized by the gurgling, clear water in which I could see schools of janga fish and the occasional shrimp; listening to the wind making music among the trees; watching the birds flitting about and scratching in the underbrush, I developed an intense relationship with nature. If love is the key, I was given the keys to the world in that sacred spot.

I finally grew into my high heels and handbag when I embarked on a quarter century of activism in the United States that has inspired thousands of people to cherish nature and each other. I served on the Board of Directors of multiple national environmental organizations, including the Board of Trustees of the National Parks Conservation Association for five three-year terms; the Board of the Association of Partners for Public Lands, (rebranded as the Public Lands Alliance); the Board of the National Parks Promotion Council; Delaware North Corporation's Parks and Resorts Diversity Advisory Committee and the Board of Directors of Chattahoochee Riverkeeper. I am a founding member and served in the leadership of the South Florida Community Partners, Keeping it Wild and Greening Youth Foundation, Atlanta.

My efforts have been recognized with numerous awards: the Marjory Stoneman Douglas Citizen Conservationist of the Year Award from the National Parks Conservation Association, 1998; the George Barley Leadership Award from the Everglades Coalition, 1998; the Environmental Hero Award from Vice President Al Gore and the National Oceanic and Atmospheric Administration, 2000; the Apex Distinguished Service Award from Black Meetings and Tourism magazine, 2014; an Orchid Award from the Miami Urban Environmental League, 2014; the Lifetime

Achievement Award from Outdoor Afro, 2016 and from CityWild 2017, among many others.

Tributes from elementary school children in Atlanta to President Barack Obama's White House show Mom had it right from the start. But what really filled me with awe and amazement at the mystery of life was when I found myself sitting at the stern of my sailboat in Florida, looking down at needlefish swimming in the river below, just as I had done on the banks of my gully in Jamaica as a little girl, watching janga in the water. Sixty years had passed, and I felt as if I had suddenly woken up from a dream.

Where had the time gone? How had I gotten to this point? I had no conscious memory of a plan or goal, and yet I was back where I started, doing the same thing I'd done as a very young child. And in the interim I'd helped to make a big difference.

I call that Destiny. I call it God. I'm so grateful for the lessons and the preparation I absorbed at my gully.

✱✱✱✱

ACKNOWLEDGEMENTS

I wish to express my gratitude to:

The Great Creator and Sustainer of Life, with whom I'm intimately connected.

My cherished husband Frank; beloved daughter Lisa Suber and her husband Ethan; our grandchildren including Frank Winston, Sydnee, Jordan, Taffrey, Jared and Camille Peterman.

My Inner Circle since age 12: Audrey Yearwood, Dorrit Nelson, Monica Melton, Cammal McCorkell and Sheena Vaccianna; and Rhemalee Fearon since our teenage years.

My besties Dr. Carolyn Finney; Carolyn Hartfield; Kate Cell, Iantha Gantt-Wright and the Diverse Environmental Leaders Speakers Bureau.

Lee Hainline and Jim Cross.

Alfred Calloway and the South Florida Community Partners.

Vintage Jamaica Facebook Group, especially Administrator Dore Tate; Greta Betty; Yvonne Provost; Beverley Gayle Barr; Hugh Campbell; Pauline Mills; Myrna Kedro; Janet Brooks-Dyer; Norka Lynch; Flo Chin; Nadia Harper; Marcia Freeman; Jean Burke; Pauline Fowler-Boggis; Dawn Fong; Sylvia Gilfillian; Gloria Shakespeare; Sheila Peart-Robinson; Dawn Chang-McGibbon; Dr. Horace James Sr. ; Tania Hernandez; Lilieth Taylor; Horace Smith, Heather Robinson, Sonia Adams and scores of others whose daily reinforcement helped me get this book done in just three months. I hope I make you proud.

My longtime friends and classmates including Desmond Palmer, Eileen Young, Bethany Powell, Carol Lopez and Hyacinth Broderick Scott who provided key vintage images.

My young cousins - the twins Jonte and Donte Johnson and brothers Geovaune and Tajoniel Thompson.

My editor Professor Elaine Douglas-Harrison; cover designer, our beloved grandson Yero Winborne and author Juju Edwards whose assistance was invaluable in producing this book.

Thank you!

****

INTRODUCTION

"Wow, Mom! That sounds like a loong time ago!! You've lived so many different lives!"

My daughter Lisa's exclamation, Sunday morning, August 25, 2019, made me burst into delighted laughter. I thought she already knew the things I was telling her about growing up in the country in Jamaica, but she was apparently hearing them for the first time. I told her how wonderful her great grandmother Ida (my Mama) was, and how amazing that, on the very day when I was planning to honor her, my friends had suddenly volunteered to take me to the beach at Rocky Point, a place that had lived in my imagination since Mama took me there as a child. That same Sunday, the United States was marking the 400th anniversary of when the first Africans were traded onto American soil, August 25, 1619. At 3 p.m. bells would begin ringing across the country to mark the event.

I told her how awesome it was that on August 1st, 20 days before my 68th birthday, my husband Frank and I were able to wade into the water at the very spot in Virginia where the Africans came ashore. We were in the company of a brilliant group of young graduates, embarking on careers as keepers of history in the National Park Service, who we'd been brought in to inspire, with the superintendent of that park, Fort Monroe National Monument, as our host. Now it looked as if I would be able to wade in the water and honor my grandma at the place in Jamaica where she first introduced me to the sea.

I reminded her that Mama was a higgler, and would occasionally take me out of primary school to go with her to the orange groves, where I would climb the trees and help her pick the fruit she bought to sell at the market in Rocky Point. Once I got to high school, Mama no longer took me to help her because she prioritized me "getting you education."

"Is a good ting you love education cause no man naw go wan' married you for you caan' do nothing," she scolded me sometimes, if I didn't do some part of the housework right. But she was very proud of her granddaughter, nicknamed Ruby after my dead aunt, and the whole village treated me like a gem. My given name is Audrey Rubina Wright.

By the time I told her about the journey on the market truck overnight Sunday to the shore, where we'd sell oranges and buy fresh fish from the fishermen coming in from the sea, then return home Monday night, Lisa was in shock. I may have finished her off when I told her that as a teenager I was expected to make dinner every Monday night when Mama was gone, for me and her and my Uncle Baugh with whom we lived. Collecting wood from outside, building the fire in the high fireplace in the bamboo wattle kitchen, kneading flour to make dumplings and peeling green bananas that stained my hands, was standard.

"Oh my God, Mom!" she blurted out. "The only cooking I had to do at that age was put a Hot Pocket in the microwave!

I was at home in Jamaica and she was at home in Atlanta. By the time we got off the phone I was committed to writing the story of my life that I'd been thinking and talking about doing for many years. In the interim I had written and published two books – the first with my husband Frank – encouraging people to discover and embrace America's National Park System and to develop a closer relationship with nature. The second is a travel guide to the national parks.

From my 68-year-old perch I can see that my life has been all about nature and communicating the inherent joy and satisfaction of cherishing the Earth. Some of my friends have found me a little kooky, but noticing life and loving it is as natural to me as breathing.

As an adult I was once walking on the beach with my close friend since childhood, Dorrit Nelson, and her family, who were visiting me in Fort Lauderdale. I was lagging behind, and noticed a yellow wildflower growing in the sand. I exclaimed with delight, which brought Dorrit running back to see what I had found. When I excitedly showed her the flower she burst out laughing.

"I thought you'd found gold or something," she said. To me it was as if I had found gold, the idea that life can grow even in the sand being another expression of the wonder of nature.

I was an only child and read voraciously. I had a crisp, mellifluent speaking voice and perfect diction, so I was often selected to make presentations that required poise and elocution. Beginning in Sunday school, continuing in high school, and accelerating when I went to work at the Gleaner Company, Jamaica's newspaper of record, I frequently had the opportunity to represent, when it was important to make a good impression.

I loved to write and to travel. In the early 1970s I was chosen to be part of the Gleaner's team traveling around the country conducting the National Spelling Bee. I got a chance to see my country from coast to coast and fell madly, passionately in love with her. Many years later when I migrated to the United States and married my soul mate, he suggested we drive around the entire country and see the highlights such as the Grand Canyon, Yellowstone and Yosemite. I enthusiastically agreed.

So when we stumbled upon America's "Crown Jewels," the system of national parks protecting the most breathtakingly scenic and historic places in the country, I was overwhelmed with love and gratitude. Then we noticed that there were literally no Black people among the employees or hundreds of thousands of visitors from around the country and the world.

First I was baffled by the disparity, and then I came to see how carefully it was maintained. The sense of equality and fairness that I absorbed growing up in Jamaica came fiercely into play. I felt duty bound to use my gifts of love and communication to help make a difference in the situation. Fortunately Frank was equally committed. The best feature of our relationship is that it's our greatest desire to make each other's dreams come true – which incidentally led to my stint as a sailor years later.

I became a speaker for the environment by default. It was the most natural thing in the world to combine the abilities exhibited from my early youth with the passion I have for nature. I started off trying to communicate the abundance of beauty in the national parks to Americans of color, and then found that it was just as necessary to educate White environmentalists about the need to engage non-White Americans with the enjoyment and protection of our sacred spaces.

Our tenacity in striving to "colorize" the park system eventually put us in the company of President Obama, United States congressmen and women, Hollywood entertainers, leaders of Fortune 100 companies, educators and the full spectrum of the American public. As independent publishers and consultants, we were never in anyone's employ, which left us free to speak our minds without fear or apology.

In 1997 when we first heard the words "climate change" and learned what it meant, a chill settled around my heart. The projections were dire and catastrophic. By then I had a biological grandson, Yero Winborne, and the gift of five other grandchildren through Frank. Thinking about the future we were creating for them made me more determined than ever to do everything I could to wake up the public. I got so overwrought that Frank not only cautioned me to take it easy, but set times when we were not allowed to talk about the environment.

"We must do all we can, but we cannot be thinking and talking about it all the time, Honey," he said.

I really tried because – I love this guy and I want to please him. I also know that obsession is not good for one's mental health.

A quarter of a century later, our names have become synonymous with leadership in the environmental sector, and many of the looming climate-related crises we raised the alarm about are now taking place. I completely understand and stand in awe of the young Swedish advocate Greta Thunberg who is at the forefront of the climate response movement. Young activists of color such as Isra Irsi, co-founder of US Youth Climate Strike, are equally committed, even if they do not get the same amount of attention.

My main goal in writing this book is to record the experiences that helped shape my life so that I could make a contribution to society. In an era of great discord in nature and humanity, I believe it is vital that each one of us takes stock of how we got to be who we are, and what we are contributing to the planet, for better or worse.

Many people seem resigned to the world ending, and some even anticipate it as their opportunity to be with God. That overlooks the hellish conditions that we are unleashing today which our descendants will have to deal with.

Frank sagely observes, "We are not trying to save the Earth. The Earth was here long before humanity, and will be here long after we're gone. What we are striving to do is to preserve the quality of the environment so that it will continue to support human life. We can't breathe concrete, nor polluted air, nor can we consume polluted water without it having a tragic effect on our health."

I remember the freshness of the air, the harmony of nature that I absorbed sitting on the banks of my gully. The atmosphere of love and acceptance predisposed me to love myself, and to strive to love others as myself. The abundance provided for our sustenance gave me faith that a benevolent God supplies all our needs and that there is enough for everyone.

I hope this book reminds us to go back to that formative place and recapture those early feelings of love and wonder. Then we may be ready to heed the Biblical injunction to "care for creation" and care for each other. Love is the answer to "saving" our world.

****

CHAPTER ONE

My earliest memory is of following my grandmother who I called Mama, down to the gully that ran behind our house to cut coco heart leaves for pepper pot soup. Mama chose the youngest shoots at the center of the plant that were still furled as they were the most tender. Mission accomplished, I walked behind her in the gully back to the house, feeling the river stones under my feet, the cool water reaching up to my ankles and flowing between my toes. I may have been three or four years old, and Mrs. Ida Butler, my Mama, was the most important person in the world to me. I imprinted on her like a duckling on its mother.

When we reached the house Mama went directly into the kitchen and began cooking dinner. The kitchen stood alone and was made of bamboo wattle and daub, with a zinc roof. The dirt floor had a slab of wood and a few crocus bags that I could sit on with my back to the wall, far enough away from the fireplace and out of Mama's way. The fireplace was elevated and consisted of three large rocks set in a triangle on top of a sheet of zinc.

To start the fire Mama brought in wood that was just the right length from outside and carefully placed some through each opening of the fireplace. Then she poured on kerosene oil and lit a match. The flames shot up practically to the ceiling, and Mama stepped back until they subsided enough for her to put on the big black heavy iron pot.

Mama was the best cook on earth. Mama was the best everything to me. Taking water out of the drum on one side of the kitchen, she filled the pot halfway with water and began peeling the breadfruit, coco, chocho, dashene and yam to put in. All of those things grew in our yard and simmered down into a delicious pepper pot soup. Mama seasoned the pot with scallion, garlic and thyme before she put in the chopped up coco leaves, the last thing before the ripe scotch bonnet pepper. That pepper gave the soup its unique flavor and she was careful not to let it burst in the pot as it would make the soup too spicy to enjoy.

Just before dusk every day except Sunday, my grandfather, Mama's husband Mr. David Butler ("Mass D"), came home. He ran the stud farm just outside Summer Field, about a mile and a half away from New Roads where we lived. He left home around sun up and walked to his job, managing huge Brahmin bulls with which farmers brought their cows to mate. Everyone including me called him Mass D, except for those who called him Missa Butler. He was a big strong handsome man and very intelligent. When he came home Mama and I waited on him hand and foot. She had his dinner ready and served it to him, and I was available to run and get anything he needed, whether it was a drink of water or a mango after dinner.

I lived with my grandparents because my mother, their daughter Bibsy, Avenel Joyce Butler, was away in Kingston working. We saw her infrequently, and I was always looking out for her. When the bus stopped at our gate and she came off with her grip, it meant we were going to have peanuts, American apples, and candy that she brought, and plenty excitement around the place. For a long time my biggest dream about growing up and going to work involved having money to buy peanuts and those apples. When Mom went back to Kingston to her job, taking care of the son of a wealthy family and their home, things went back to normal.

Dusk brought neighbors to our house, mostly women who sat on the verandah with Mama and talked, while their children and I played under the cellar. Our house was made of concrete and sat on stilts, the back held up by tall concrete poles. The front was a short drop down from the main road and occupied the few feet of level ground before the land fell away. The opening created by the back hanging into space was the favorite playground for my friends and me, if we couldn't be in the gully.

The gully was the key feature of the place, a sweet babbling stream with clear cool water. I was lucky enough to have a "deep hole" behind our house, a spot where the gully bed dropped down into a depression, with a sandy bottom and only a few rocks. This made it the perfect swimming spot and, as if I didn't already have every inducement for my house to be the most popular place with the other children, I also had a mango tree growing above the swimming hole that dropped mangoes into the water. It was the variety named "common" mango maybe because they were so plentiful. They grew big and fat and sweet and as soon as they started turning color, we started throwing rocks at them to knock them down. I'd race my friends to grab mangoes that came bobbing downstream, and there was always enough for everyone.

We ate mangoes when we got hungry outside of breakfast and dinner time, along with oranges and ortaniques, "stangerines," jelly water coconut, naseberries, guavas and rose apples which grew abundantly on Mass D's property sloping up the hill. The orange trees bore profusely and we consumed the oranges liberally. We all had our favorite trees that bore the sweetest fruit, but my hands-down favorite was the Ugly fruit tree. First of all, how could one call a fruit ugly? Secondly, the bumpy thick skin cradled the biggest slices of the juiciest citrus. Pure nectar.

The gully met all our needs for bathing and washing clothes, but for drinking water we went to the spring. A group of children would make plans to go together and we looked forward to it. I took my bucket up to the road where I joined the other children, and we walked happily down the main road laughing and joking. Below Mass Rennie's house on the hill we turned right, walking through the dense coffee bushes with leaves so thick they seemed to absorb all the light. We came out in a clearing where fresh cool water gushed out of a rock and pooled beneath. I filled my bucket and hoisted it onto my head, looking forward to the day I'd be able to balance it without holding on, as the older children did.

When I was born, Mass D planted my navel string (umbilical cord) under a breadfruit tree at the edge of his property near my godfather Mass Val Fearon's property. The tree and I were intended to grow together, and to this day it is still standing strong and bearing prized Yellow Heart breadfruit. I visited it shortly after I started writing this story and was proud to see this living talisman of my entire life still thriving.

Mass Val was a tall, handsome light-skinned man, and his best feature to me was that he had a daughter named Monica, my god sister. Monica was delicate and beautiful with long curly black hair and, since I was a year older, I was very protective of her. Every school day we held hands and walked the half mile or so to the school that was held in our church, the Church of God.

My favorite part of school was recess and lunch time. After lunch the teachers put us to sleep on towels on the pulpit. By the time they woke us up I was ready to go home. Years later when I went to high school my friends teased me that I only came to school for break time and lunch. What's the problem with that, I joked.

The only uncomfortable part of life was the pit toilet, positioned on the opposite side of the house from the kitchen. Every house in the village had a pit toilet but it would take a dire emergency to make me get out of bed at night to go to the toilet by myself, carrying a tin lamp for visibility in the pitch black darkness. For lesser needs we kept a chimmy pot under the bed, and it was my duty to empty it in the morning, then wash and replace it.

Our lives were blissfully innocent and very real. We kept chickens in the yard and collected the eggs they laid under the cellar. On a Saturday afternoon I might help Mama hold the pan over a chicken's flapping body so she could cleanly cut its head off. Some Saturday mornings my grandfather and his friends might kill a pig or goat in the backyard, and everybody in the neighborhood came to get a piece of meat. They kept a fire burning to help with the skinning, as they poured boiling water over the slain pig to make it easier to remove the hairs. They'd cut out the liver and the sweetbread, roast them on the fire and share them among us children.

Mama and Mass D and all the adults firmly believed in God, and church was as much a place to educate children as school. Until I was about 16, I went to church three times on Sunday - 8 a.m. for Sunday School, 11 a.m. for Sunday Service and 7 p.m. for Sunday Night Service. Monday night at 7 p.m. we went to Prayer Service, Wednesday was Bible Study and Friday night, Young People's Meeting. As soon as I was a "grown up" working in Kingston and sharing a house with two of my girlfriends, I stopped going to church. My relationship with God was already firmly established.

They say a person's character and personality are formed by age 7, and the trajectory of your life set. "It takes a village to raise a child," and I was raised by such a village. As a fish swimming in my gully doesn't know what is supplying its needs, I had no idea that I was the beneficiary of love and caring on the scale of a whole community. I did not know I was loved because someone told me, as no one spoke of love. Nor did I know how sheltered and protected I was, though I was free to roam anywhere with my friends. All the adults looked out for all the children, and that was the norm. I lived in a cocoon of happiness and security and I didn't know anything else existed.

Until the night I woke up to hear Mass D beating Mama. I lay there for a while, disbelieving my ears. Then I jumped out of bed and flew into their room where I began raining blows on his legs with my balled-up little fists. I had never heard or seen him hit Mama before, and he'd never hit me, but now he took off his belt and gave me several lashes on my rump.

"If you were bigger you'd be beating me up for your Mama," he said.

I was seven years old. The following day passed in a blur. Mass D did not stay home from his important job at the stud farm. That gave Mama time to plan, because in the middle of the next night she woke me up quietly.

"Get up. We're leaving," she whispered.

Huh? Leaving? Going where? My mind churned with questions, but I got dressed and we crept out into the night. It was pitch black. Mama had a bottle lamp with kerosene in the bottle and a cloth wick. We waited by the side of the road and sometime later a vehicle arrived and picked us up.

I never knew what set Mass D off and Mama never talked about it. I suspect it had something to do with the lady he brought in from another parish a few months later. She was a teacher and when I met her I felt shocked that anyone could choose someone over Mama who was much more beautiful. I heard rumors that Mass D said he needed an educated woman for his wife.

I'd learned the creation story in church and now I could see that, even in the midst of a seemingly idyllic life, things were not perfect. There was indeed that proverbial "snake" of deceit and violence. But Mama showed me that you don't have to accept abuse and suffer, that you can make a different choice. I learned that I had options and, no matter what, I would choose the option that kept me free and happy. For more than 60 years that confidence has served me exceptionally well.

CHAPTER TWO

I found out when we arrived that our new home would be with Uncle Baugh, Mama's cousin on her mother's side. He lived in Rose Hill closer to Summer Field, in a two-room house on a hill above the road. His yard was full of orange and ortanique trees and he had a kitchen a little ways higher than the house. We were on the opposite side of the road from my beloved gully, just a short sprint down the hill, across the road and through Brother Sam's yard.

The best feature of our new home was that it was next door to Mama's cousin Brother Reggie Thomas, who had a houseful of children who became my closest playmates. A truck driver who mainly came home on weekends, he had a beautiful wife named Henrietta that he met in Mocho. She had three children and together they had four other children, which gave me a plethora of cousins to play with. I spent more time in their yard than in mine.

They had a huge cashew tree and our favorite pastime on Saturday evenings was to roast hundreds of cashews in a fiery pyre, break them open and eat them burning hot. On Sunday afternoons Brother Reggie liked to load up the open-backed truck with all the village children and take us for a "drive out." I fell in love with traveling, as I always expected to see something wonderful and new around the next corner.

In Rose Hill Mama was closer to her family and seemed happier for it. All down the road into town someone from her family lived, starting with the shopkeeper Brother Cecil and his wife Miss Mulvena who were our cousins, just as Jane and Blanche and others down the street were our cousins. I don't know how Mama and Mass D wound up in New Roads as I don't recall meeting anyone from Mass D's family there. Since he had the house and land it must have been convenient to settle there.

Uncle Baugh was truly a unique human being. He was very tall and thin and moved slowly and deliberately. He spoke little and never laughed, and I never saw him with a woman. He was kind to Mama and me, and when something happened that caused my cousin Errol who was about my age to have to come and live with us for a while, he did not object.

Mama and Errol and I slept in one room, in one double bed, with a table bearing a glass lamp with the words "Home Sweet Home" on the lampshade, and a table in the corner where we kept our groceries. Errol's parents in England sent for him soon after and it was back to Mama and me.

To support us, Mama became an entrepreneur. A market truck passed through our neighborhood every Sunday night, anytime from around 6 p.m. to 9 or 10 a.m. Monday morning, if it had broken down. It carried "higglers," mostly women but a few men, to Rocky Point on the Caribbean coast where they sold ground provisions such as yam and green bananas, as well as fruits including oranges, and bought fish to bring back and sell in their communities.

Mama decided to become a higgler. She bought oranges from neighboring landowners which involved climbing the tree and picking them on Fridays or Saturdays, filling big crocus bags and leaving them at the side of the road Sunday evening. Many times I went with her to pick oranges and I loved the adventure. I was a very thin child so I could climb out onto the farthest branches and press them down so she could pick the sweet ripe oranges.

I loved the times she took me with her to Rocky Point. That Sunday night we'd go to bed fully dressed and listening out for the sound of the truck horn. The driver knew where each higgler lived and would sound the horn stridently to make sure they were ready and took as little time as possible to get loaded up.

We were one of the last stops on that road, so by the time the truck got to us it was usually full. Everyone knew each other and the adults sitting on flat, backless wooden benches would squeeze up closer together and make room for Mama. My place was to sit on one of the bags on the truck floor and make myself comfortable. If it was nighttime people mostly tried to get some sleep, but if the truck was late and we were traveling in daylight, there'd be much conversation with the truck sidemen explaining what happened and the higglers bemoaning how they'd miss their regular fishermen.

Occasionally there were other children on the truck, and we'd be the first to jump off and run down to the sea when we reached Rocky Point. The sidemen unloaded the big bags of goods and the higglers lugged them to their spot in the market. It truly was a whole community as the newcomers exchanged pleasantries with the higglers who were already there. We children could run around the market and our parents had no concern because they taught us good sense and they knew everyone was looking out for us.

After a full day of selling and buying, storing the fish on ice, it would be time to get back on the truck for the return trip. The timing depended, I think, on the driver's confidence in his vehicle and whether or not his truck was reliable - you wouldn't want to break down at night in the dark. The atmosphere going back was even more languid as everyone was worn out from the day.

On Tuesday mornings Mama set up shop at the farthest corner of the property under a tamarind tree. She had regular customers and she knew what each one wanted so she would gut, scale and clean three pounds of snapper for this customer, some doctor fish for that one and some parrot or goat fish for another. Several people came to the yard to get their fish, and I was responsible for distributing the rest. Mama sold on the "trus'" system, which meant the people got the fish on Tuesdays, then paid for it on Friday or Saturday, validating her trust.

In turn Mama "trussed" groceries from Brother Cecil. She often sent me to get staples such as flour, cornmeal, sugar, rice and salt. Brother Cecil would measure out the items from behind the counter and count up how much the bill came to. He'd write that on a pink ticket and stick it on the nail that had scores of similar tickets. On Saturdays Mama paid up.

Once I started high school Mama stopped letting me go with her to pick oranges. I still had to collect the fish money though, which meant I'd go to the door of a family that had children in my class, and stand on their doorstep with my hand out. Often my classmates would come to the door to pay me. Somehow it made our relationship feel less equal, and I didn't realize that it created a psychological problem for me until much later in my life.

In Rose Hill I still had my gully. It was deeper and more secluded than in New Roads, and I was often the only person there. I'd sit near the edge of the bank where I could see the largest expanse of water from curve to curve. I loved to watch the fish swimming leisurely or darting, chasing each other. The little janga fish traveled in schools and made delightful curves in the water. Occasionally I saw an eel come out from under the bank and into the current, or a pretty pink shrimp propel itself on its tail from one spot to another. The fish looked huge to me. (When I went back as an adult I saw they were minnows. How did that happen?)

The breeze came through the trees and fanned me. The shadows changed position on the water as the sun shifted. The birds called and scratched in the underbrush – I absorbed all of nature in almost a dream state.

I had my own pig. Many of my friends had animals that we were expected to take care of to learn responsibility. I loved my pig, and always took it down to the gully and tied it out where it could reach water and feast on water grass, a succulent grass with a blue flower that pigs love. I did that every morning before going to school. One day I was chopping wood to make the fire to boil my pig's food, mostly breadfruit with the skin still on. I was chopping with gusto and chopped my left thumb almost clean off. Paralyzed for a moment by the blood spurting and half my thumb flopping off, I screamed and ran to Mama splashing blood everywhere. She calmly held my thumb and put it back together, cut some aloe and put the gel on it, then bandaged it in a rag. Thankfully, it healed with no scar.

I wasn't quite as lucky when the pig bit me. I don't know what set it off, but one morning I was walking past when it lunged and bit me. It wasn't hard enough to take out a chunk but it gave me a long deep scratch on the bone at the front of my left leg. I screamed like a hyena and Mama cleaned my wound and bandaged it. I never knew what happened to the pig but, by the time I came home from school, it was gone.

Part of my duties as a "bright" child was to write letters for the older people. My favorite was Sister Sam, the estranged wife of Brother Sam. Sister Sam had several daughters abroad who wrote to her regularly, the letters coming by air mail on a blue fold-over paper made just for that purpose, marked *Par Avion*. I loved writing for Sister Sam because she prefaced every sentence with, "Tell her seh me seh fe tell her seh...." Midway through writing the last sentence, I'd ask her for the next one, in order to give her time to finish the preamble.

Sister Sam had a sister named Aunt Cordella who lived past New Roads in Beckford Kraal. Aunt Cordella was the candy lady – she made and sold white peppermint candies with red stripes. Sometimes she'd take me home with her and we made candy, boiling the mixture, allowing it to cool and then twisting it and cutting it into bite-sized pieces. I got to eat some while it was still warm. Oh joy!

Mama could take ANYTHING and make it into a delectable dish. She was so generous that she always cooked a big pot of food for just me and her and Uncle Baugh – in case someone dropped by. One couple dropped by almost every day around dinner time, and Mama never tired of feeding them. When I started going to high school, four of my best friends (Monica, Dorrit, Cammal and Audrey) loved to come home with me on Tuesday evenings when they knew Mama had cooked up a feast of fresh fish. Then they'd laugh that they were going home to eat their own dinner. It was a treat for me and Mama, and from that I absorbed the feeling that there was always enough, and there would always be more.

Mama's "flabba," a concoction that used flour and flaked salt fish to hold together green field peas, was one of my favorite dishes. Meat was mostly pork, chicken or goat, and mostly consumed on Sundays.

Our neighborhood had some very colorful people, especially Mass Ding Dong and Miss Magnel. Ding Dong was the village bad man, about six feet tall and well built, very loud and boisterous and always in trouble. Ding Dong was often quarreling with someone and threatening to fight them and beat them up. Miss Magnel who lived next door to him weighed maybe 90 pounds, and she was usually trying to hold him back.

"You betta hold me, Magnel! You betta hold me or I will beat his...," Ding Dong roared.

When the altercation was resolved without a punch being thrown he'd say, "If Magnel neva hol' me back you see...! I woulda..."

Ding Dong was a constant source of entertainment for us children.

Brother Reggie's family had a radio at his house that I could hear from my house, and every morning when the DJ played "If you see the rooster running, 16 sexy chicken chasing him, round and round the corner," I knew that meant it was time to start getting ready for school.

In Rose Hill we children went to the standpipe near Brother Cecil's shop to get water, bring it home on our head, pour it into a drum or a barrel and go back for more. Our conversations were spiced with fun and laughter as we walked to the pipe and back. By now I could carry my bucket on my head without needing to hold it. But one day I slipped as I was hoisting it and it hit me on my head, splitting my skull. I had to be rushed to the hospital about two miles away in Chapelton where I got stitches, I think without benefit of anesthetic because it hurt so much. To this day I can feel the scar in my head.

My all-time favorite activity was going to mango bush. All the neighborhood children would make a plan to meet at dawn on Saturday and go to mango bush together. We didn't have clocks so we must have been tuned into sunrise, because we all arrived at our meeting spot around the same time.

We walked to mango bush, a place typically bearing acres of mango trees that must have been communal property, because I never heard of anyone owning it nor did anyone ever object to us reaping mangoes by the score. We arrived as the sun was just beginning to pierce through the leaves and reveal the biggest, most luscious-looking fruit. Heaven on earth!

There were many varieties of mangoes including Common mangoes, Number Eleven, Blackie, Julie, Hayden, and Millie. My greatest thrill was to come upon a big fat pretty ripe mango that had just fallen into the bed of soft leaves under the tree, still firm and perfect with the stem wet from where it had been attached. I'd put that big mango in my face and bite into it, the warm juice running down my chin, through my fingers and down my arms. The sounds of children finding and eating mangoes and putting them in our baskets rang through mango bush. We walked back home desultorily on a sugar high, filled to the gills with mango juice.

We played marbles and jacks, jumped rope made from vines we called "wiss," played hide and seek, ring-a-round the roses and hula hoop. We picked guavas and cherries, rose apples and jimbelin, cut sugar cane and picked water coconut off the tree, for a never-ending supply of goodies to eat. Jackfruit and "Tinkin Toe" were notorious for their pungent smell and we had to be very careful not to choke on the powdery Tinkin Toe or hasham, a powder made by beating roasted corn in a mortar.

A duty I loved was to go to the river to wash clothes. One day a week, Mama and some of the village ladies and children would pack all our dirty clothes into round bath pans made of tin, carry them on our head and walk about three quarters of a mile through town to the river on the outskirts of town. There was a bridge over the river and we went down the side onto the very rocky shore – about three times as wide as the river. Picking our way through the rocks down to the water we'd all set our wash pans down off our head. The adults would choose what big rock they'd sit on for the day while all the children ran screaming and splashing in the river. Our parents would call us back to bring water to fill up their bath pans and they'd start washing the white clothes first and lay them out on the rocks to bleach.

Every family had a "clappa stick" made of wood with a narrow handle carved out so you could get a good grip. We used it to "beat" the dirt out of the clothes, placing them wet and soapy on a rock and smacking them several times with the clappa stick, then rinsing the clothes out in the water and beating them a few more times. The children were responsible for doing some of the wash, and when we finished we were free to spend the rest of the day playing in the river.

When the adults finished washing and rinsing, they'd "blue" the white clothes in a solution made with a cube of blue and lots of water. It was supposed to make the whites brighter. At the end of the wash day we packed up the clothes – mostly dry but some still damp – and carried them back home where we hung them out on the clothes line.

The following day or some day after would be time to starch and iron the clothes. We made starch from cassava, which was also eaten boiled or processed into delicious bammies. To make starch we grated the cassava, diluted it with water and strained the mixture, squeezing out the pulpy mass and leaving just the liquid. Then we'd put that in the sun for hours until it dried into a chalky substance.

Next we'd "draw" the starch which required putting just the right small amount into a pan and pouring boiling water on it while stirring so that there were minimal lumps. Then we'd run that through a soft cloth to make sure the sticky mixture was perfectly smooth. Finally we'd dunk the clothes that needed to be starched in it so that it was saturated, wring it out and hang it on the clothesline. If a lump got into the mixture it might lodge in a garment and create an unsightly blotch, requiring that we wash it all over again.

(Years later when one of my American girlfriends was complaining about having to do laundry which consists of putting clothes in a machine and turning a knob, placing it in a dryer and spraying on starch from a can, I told her what doing laundry used to mean to me. She begged me to stop, saying it made her tired just to hear it.)

Ironing meant making up a fire in a circular stove from wood we had burned into coal. Our family had four flat, triangular irons that we set up on the stove with their tips touching. The irons got very hot and had a film of ash on their face. We used some thick old cloth to hold them and take them off the stove, and then we'd rub the surface on some other old material to clean them off. Finally they'd be ready to iron the clothes which we'd have sprinkled with water and wrapped up to keep them moist and supple. When I started going to high school and had two pairs of uniforms it was one of my greatest challenges to keep my uniforms freshly pressed each day and ready for school next morning.

Occasionally we went to collect wood to burn and make coal. We left at dawn in a group and walked about two miles to Pennants where we picked up wood, mostly from the logwood tree, which was very good for burning. Once we took a donkey to carry the wood and, as I was the smallest, someone put me in one of the two hampers attached to the donkey. Before they could put something or someone else in the other hamper to balance it, the donkey took off galloping down the road with me hanging on for dear life. Behind me people were running after the donkey and screaming for it to stop, but the donkey had other ideas. Luckily someone coming from the opposite direction was able to grab the rope around its neck and slow it down.

I don't remember being scared, and maybe that's where my tendency comes from not to be scared. In any situation I do all I can to achieve the outcome I want, but once it's out of my hands I relax completely. It's the same when I get on an airplane, a roller coaster or the Goodyear Blimp which I've had the good fortune to ride on. From a donkey to the blimp - what a great life!

****

CHAPTER THREE

All the neighborhood children went to the Church of God. The Baptist church was a place of ebullient worship where people sang and danced and prayed loudly. The sisters especially would often catch the Spirit and leap out of their seats to dance in the aisles. I played the cymbal and Monica and I were very enthusiastic participants. Once we got so inspired that we both went up at altar call to accept Christ as our Lord and Savior. As we were walking down the aisle some of the ladies reached out and placed a covering over our head to show respect for the Lord. As young Christians we were not allowed to sing along with secular music on the radio and we were expected to dress very modestly with our hems below our knees. Within two weeks we were backsliders as we couldn't live up to the requirements.

When I was around age 11, a new church called The Assemblies of God appeared in the village. I told Mama I wanted to start going to that church. Many of my friends told their parents the same thing. Our parents and guardians were very indulgent with us and let us go, even though they continued to go to the Church of God.

We had the same number of services but our pastor Brother Foster was very charismatic, and his wife Sister Foster was a gentle though sickly lady. They had a son named Lloyd who became my first crush.

When I was about 12, I noticed something in church that would shape the course of my life. Brother Foster could speak in tongues and, while it sounded like a mish mash of unintelligible words, I noticed that when he spoke in tongues there would be an electric charge in the air, as if something could ignite and explode. Other members would begin speaking in tongues as well, and some of the sisters would stand up and jump and dance in the aisles while speaking in tongues and praising God.

As a child I observed this in wonder. But what struck me most of all was that when Brother Foster came out of his trance and translated what he'd said in tongues, he used words of multiple syllables in complete grammatical syntax. He sounded like a highly educated teacher, although in regular life he spoke the same patois and broken English that most Jamaicans use.

How did he do that? I never stopped wondering, though I never asked. Children were not encouraged to question adults. I interpreted it to mean that there is a world just beyond us, separated by a veil we cannot see, that we can enter into and bring back information and inspiration. For my whole life since then, when I hear people talk about whether or not they believe that there is a God, I smile. Whatever you choose to call it, whether you believe it exists or not, does not affect the fact that it IS. This has been the greatest source of security, assurance and optimism in my life, because I was programmed to believe that the Unseen is working lovingly on my behalf, and it has never failed me.

I attended Chapelton Primary School along with all my friends in the neighborhood. We walked in groups of two or three the few miles to school, walking up Trafalgar Hill which was very steep. Occasionally my father would be driving by, going in the same direction, and he'd pick us up and take us to Chapelton. The possibility that he or his brother my Uncle Boss might come by in their cars and give us a ride, gave me a certain cachet among my friends.

On our way home from school we'd use the last of the day's allowance to go to the bakery and buy fresh-baked cush bread or bulla cake - a sweet round cake that goes perfectly with cheese or avocado. We'd hold off on eating until we passed through town and were on Trafalgar Hill, and then we'd dive in. Once my father came by and caught me and my friends eating on the road. He chastised me soundly and basically said it was a sign of poor breeding to eat on the road. I was so embarrassed I never did it again, even as an adult.

At the bottom of Trafalgar Hill was a house with an Otaheite apple tree in the front yard. In season, the owners sometimes let us climb the tree and pick the sweet, succulent red fruit. Similar to rose apples, they have a very exotic taste. Climbing that tree and getting those luscious apples was a sweet spot in our lives.

At age 11 in elementary school at Chapelton Primary, I got to take the exam to go to Clarendon College ("CC"), the local high school. Along with all the other children I waited with bated breath for the exam results to come out. They were published in the Daily Gleaner and took up several pages of the broadsheet newspaper. I found my name, but it was in the column for people who got "half scholarship." That meant my family would have to pay part of my tuition, along with books and other necessities. My father said no, that I needed to remain in primary school and take the exam again.

Until I reached high school age, I had only a passing relationship with my father Joseph Wright, whom everyone called Massa Wright. He lived on the other side of town where the wealthier people lived, and owned both a car and a truck. That put him probably among the top 10 wealthiest people in our community. He lived with his wife who was a dressmaker and had no children.

I gathered that my father as a grownup had a dalliance with my beautiful young mother when she was only 16, and I was the product of that. People on our side of town treated me with particular respect because first, I was Massa Wright's daughter; second, I was Miss Ida's granddaughter; third, I was Mister Butler's granddaughter; and last of all, I was very bright. It was a given that I would become somebody.

Fortunately in January 1964, at age 12, I won a full scholarship and entered Clarendon College in Form 1C. This changed the trajectory of my life again. It was the only high school in relatively close proximity to us, the closest others in Clarendon being Glenmuir in May Pen, 13 country miles away, and Vere Tech which was even farther away. It would have been an extreme hardship for my family to afford to send me to one of those schools, if not a total impossibility.

Now I am grateful to my dad for his decision, because entering school that year gave me the best lifelong friends a girl could ever have. Six of us who met in First Form have remained friends our entire lives.

My closest friends were Cammal Buddan, who came from a community beyond May Pen and boarded at Miss Hilda's house on the street where my father lived. Dorrit Brown came from Mullet Hall, and she was close friends with Audrey Folkes from Coxswain. Many mornings they walked together almost five miles over rutted unpaved roads, through cane fields and orange groves, and arrived at school with not a hair out of place, looking like they'd just stepped off the cover of a fashion magazine. Dorrit was the leader of our little clique, and we'd surround her like little ducklings, laughing at her jokes as we walked to Chapelton on our lunchtime. She grew up to be a prominent figure on Wall Street who once rang the opening bell, a privilege granted to very few people. She also co-founded the influential organization, Women on Wall Street (WOWS), and visited more than 80 countries and all seven continents.

The other star in our orbit was Sheena Grandison. Where Dorrit was tall and elegant, Sheena was petite and very chic. She had a wicked sense of humor and was incredibly precocious. Once we were in a history class in Fifth Form, and our very proper teacher Mrs. Peryer said something about a bull cow.

"Excuse me Mrs. Peryer," Sheena piped up. "There's no such thing as a bull cow. It's either a bull or a cow. It can't be both."

With that, Mrs. Peryer sent her packing, ordering her to leave the class.

As she flounced out the door Sheena said, "Well, I don't care what you people think about me, you know. Because when I get home, my family is going to love me just the same."

Wow! I had never imagined such temerity, that one could speak to an adult in that manner, much less a teacher! And the world didn't come crashing down! So I extrapolated from it that I too, could choose to be self-determining. I didn't have to try to conform or get along so that everyone would like me. It was one of the most liberating lessons of my life. It served me extraordinarily well later in America when I was sitting at Board tables with the leaders of Fortune 100 companies and other billionaires. I could hold my own with anyone.

Though she was a year younger, my god sister Monica came to school the same year as me. Fortunately my friends from the village also entered high school at the same time. Evelyn Bloomfield and Annie Williams lived a little farther up the road. Evelyn would call for Annie as she passed her house, then they'd both call for me. We laughed and talked the entire mile and a half walk to school, taking a short cut that led us past my father's house, along the train lines and through the guava bush. I loved trying to walk along the iron rails, placing one foot carefully ahead of the other. I'm certain it helped me develop balance.

When it was guava time all the children going that way picked as many of the luscious ripe fruit as we wanted. As the smallest I got to climb out onto the farthest branches and push them down so my friends could pick the topmost guavas.

The story of Clarendon College is legendary. The school was the brainchild of the Rev. Lester Davy, a minister of the United Church in Jamaica and the Cayman Islands. Rev. Davy was reportedly such an ardent follower of Christ that when he saw a poor, sick man living under some coconut thatch branches, completely at the mercy of the elements, he told his congregation to find the man a place to live or he would leave the pastorage and go and live with him. If the conditions were unsuitable for a Christian pastor, he said, then they were unsuitable for any child of God. His determination was so strong that the congregation had to speedily build a hut for the destitute man.

Observing the paucity of educational opportunities in the parish, Rev. Davy reached out to some of the luminaries in his circle and told them he planned to start a school for the children of the poor farmers.

"I shall light a candle in Chapelton, whose flame shall never be put out," he declared.

The school opened on February 2, 1942 with a robust curriculum and eight devoted teachers, including Mrs. Hyacinth Peryer who'd bought into Rev. Davy's dream.

Just three weeks later, Rev. Davy was on the train to Kingston to buy an engagement ring for his fiancée and books for the school, when his train was hit by another and he was killed instantly. But the candle he lit survived that devastating event, as the other teachers nurtured and fanned the flame.

When I got to be the guest speaker at the 75th Anniversary Founders' Day Celebration in 2017, I told approximately 1,000 young people gathered in the auditorium that the best life they could live was to emulate the selflessness of our benefactor and to do for others whatever they can. As a beneficiary of such a loving and proud tradition, words fail to convey the depth of appreciation and gratitude that I have for this institution. It is so ideally situated that when Frank visited the campus with me and saw the vista spreading in almost a full circle below us, vivid with African tulip trees in full orange bloom and riotous color everywhere, he marveled,

"This reminds me of the open-air campus Socrates talked about, perched up here on a hill overlooking such a panorama."

The Principal in 1964 when I entered, Mr. C.L. Stuart, was a short gentleman, with a quiet poise and elegance. Fondly known as "Pops," his appearance and the way he carried himself commanded instant respect. When he spoke he cast a spell.

"He who runs against time has an antagonist not subject to casualty," he intoned to the assembled student body every morning at Devotions. Fifty-five years later, graduates from that time still recite that injunction solemnly and burst into laughter when we get together.

The other half of the Stuart team was Mrs. Stuart whom everyone lovingly called "Moms." She was the Home Economics teacher and a mother to all the students, particularly the girls. I barely held my own in Home Economics, though I was considered bright in other subjects. English was my strong suit and I had a mellifluent speaking voice. Starting in First Form, I was often chosen to make the presentation to a departing teacher or anything that involved speaking before the entire school. Once a young lady in Sixth Form became quite irritated that "this little grub" – the common name for students in the lower forms – was given such a privilege.

Around this time in my high school years, my dad began to take a real interest in me. He played dominoes at the Chapelton Police Station with the officers and some of the teachers from school. Whenever he heard that I had done something extraordinary, he would drive to our house and stop on the road below and blow his horn for me to come down. I'd run down the hill to greet him and he'd tell me he'd heard something good about me and that I should keep up the good work.

It was also the only time he gave me money, so I came to associate doing outstanding work with getting money. This presented a huge problem for me later in my life because when I kept getting plaudits and awards I expected money to follow, and it never did. Only much later did I learn that in the United States you have to attach value to what you do and make it clear that you expect to be paid.

I had no inclination toward Math or Science, and became something of a novelty to my friends when I decided to just let it go and focus on what I was good at. They looked askance at me when I showed up for a big Geometry test without my Geometry set. I was a great debater and a star on the debate team, and I wrote essays that were sometimes read to the entire student body.

As Clarendon College was a boarding school there was a hierarchy. At the top were the boarders and then the day students. We were organized into "houses" and had a strong sports program – including football, netball and track and field. On Sports Day the houses adorned their mascots with rosettes in their house colors, and twice Monica was the mascot for our Harvey House. My talent was running, though I was not fast enough to be competitive and I did not compete in any sport. I don't know if it's related, but I lack the competitive gene and for that I am very grateful.

The festivities of Sports Day were usually rounded off with a movie shown for the entire school. Young lovers paired up under the watchful eyes of our teacher chaperones, being careful not to be seen touching. It was often an Elvis Presley movie and I loved him until I heard that he said the only thing a Black person could do for him was clean his shoes. After that I didn't care to see him anymore.

My "boyfriend" Lloydie, Brother Foster's stepson, did not go to Clarendon College, so he waited for me near the bottom of the hill when my friends and I came down. Once when we got to the turn off to go up the hill to my house, he tilted my face up and kissed me. It was my first kiss and I fell into a blissful trance. Then I heard someone clear their throat. Sitting on the bank above us was Ding Dong, and he was making sure we knew he was there.

I was never more mortified in my life, and for weeks I lived in fear that he would tell my grandmother. Luckily that never happened, and he never tried to hold it over my head. Pretty soon

Lloydie moved on to an older girl who didn't go to CC, giving me my first taste of heartbreak.

Periodically a group of us would skip classes and go down to the river for a picnic. Music and food were the order of the day as we splashed around and behaved just like teenagers. Some of the older boys, such as Butch Diah and Conover Jones, ran things, making sure we had music and food and drinks in abundance. Butch was also a sports star and came from a prominent family, and he and Cammal were the school's most popular couple. They got married soon after graduation and had two brilliant sons, Maxmillian and Philip, both of whom serve with the US Military, Max as Staff Sergeant in the Air Force and Philip as Senior Chief Fire Controlman in the Navy.

I passed five of the eight subjects I took at O Levels, with a distinction in English. This was commonly the time when many young people left school and went to work to earn income and help their families. I saw an ad in the Daily Gleaner that the paper was looking to hire sub-editors. I eagerly applied and was among six people chosen from a pool of hundreds that took the test. My happiness knew no bounds. I was done with school!

I moved to Kingston to live with my mother and work at the Gleaner. It was a whole new world. I had traveled the 50 miles to Kingston on the country bus many times while I was in high school to spend school holidays with Mom. But it was an entirely different thing to live with her and to be a working woman. My mother was far more authoritative than Mama which made it tense for me to be around her. My friend Audrey also came to stay with us for a while.

By then I had a boyfriend named Edgar who was much older than me, still living in Clarendon. I was missing him, so he and I made a plan that I would come to May Pen and he would pick me up there. I persuaded Audrey to back me up when we told my mom that we were going to visit Audrey's dad in Ocho Rios one Saturday morning. Instead we took the bus to May Pen and had a great time with Edgar, going out to eat and hang out, after which he drove us back to Kingston.

Next morning Mom asked,

"How was the trip to Ochie?"

"Great!" I raved. "We had such a good time with Mr. Folkes and Audrey's family."

"So how did you like Fern Gully?" she said

"Fern Gully?" I responded blankly. "I didn't see it. I must have been sleeping when we went past it."

"You were sleeping going and coming?" she persisted.

I was totally flustered, and so was Audrey. Thankfully, Mom let the subject drop, and we breathed a sigh of relief.

The following morning she started up again.

"I called Mr. Folkes and he said he never saw you guys, you never came to visit him."

Busted! Just like that, I cracked. I confessed everything on the spot.

Mom burst out laughing.

"You two think you can fool me? You think I was born yesterday? I never called Mr. Folkes but I could tell you were lying to me."

Oh, the agony. From that moment on, I made up my mind I would never tell another lie in my life. I might not tell the whole story, but I definitely will not lie. It's too demeaning when you're found out.

I worked three months at the Gleaner as a copy editor on the Star newspaper under the famous Jack Anderson. Then I decided to go back to school and take the A Level exams. I'd made lots of friends at the Gleaner, and both Mr. Anderson and Managing

Editor Mr. Theodore Sealy told me to come back when I finished school.

****

CHAPTER FOUR

I returned to Clarendon College feeling very sophisticated since I'd been a working woman and moreover worked at the prestigious Gleaner Company. I wore my hair natural and had it cut in a fashionable Miriam Makeba style. I expected to be greeted as a worldly fashion plate. Imagine my surprise when the other students laughed at my hair and made fun of me! This was not an experience I'd had before or ever expected, so I decided I was never going to school again.

Monica and Cammal stepped up and said you have to go to school, so let's go to Kingston and buy you a wig. I had some money saved from my working days, so the three of us took the bus to Kingston, went downtown and got me fitted with a long-haired wig. I couldn't manage it by myself, so every morning Evelyn or Annie would come to my house and help me fix it into a passable style. I was so relieved when my hair grew back!

The next two years passed in a blur. I was a member of the 4-H Club, the Debating Society, the Drama Club and Editor of the school magazine. In 1970 I graduated and went back to work at the Gleaner full time.

Once again I was working with Mr. Anderson who loved nothing more than to go to the bar with his friends. He was very easygoing and a good teacher but, where he was easy, his self-appointed second Mr. Davis, an older gentleman who'd recently returned from England, was hell on wheels. He was very "speaky spokey," very proper, very authoritative and supercilious.

The Gleaner began publication in 1834, the year slavery was abolished in Jamaica. It was highly respected in the way you respect your elders. The Star, a salacious tabloid also published by The Gleaner Company, was loved in a more familiar way, like a friend.

Editor-in-Chief Mr. Sealy filled me and the entire staff with awe. I never heard one person say a bad word about him. He'd walk through the office ramrod straight, shoulders back, every strand of his curly gray hair brushed back and in place. When his glance fell on you, you felt very special. Each one of us was on our best behavior when he was around, even the more militant reporters.

Barbara Gloudon, Editor of the Star, was a vivid contrast to Mr. Sealy. Where he was reserved, she was exuberant and more flamboyant. She created the column "Stella" that ran on Saturdays in the Star, and everyone looked forward to her labrish in patois. She spanned the country's political, social and international life. Once when she was interviewed on TV by the legendary journalist David Frost, who was trying to show his superior intelligence, she turned the tables on him completely, being so gentle and sweet yet pointed. He got so flustered that she patted him gently on the knee to calm him down. I thought she was the most brilliant, accomplished woman on Earth. Years later when my colleagues on national Boards told me, "Oh Audrey, you start off so sweet and complimentary and then you place the dagger," I knew it began with her example.

"Mrs. G," as we called her, was my boss on the Star where I worked as a sub-Editor alongside a talented group of young people, including: Lolita Tracey, a leggy beauty from Spanish Town; dapper Howard McGowan who'd lived in the States and spoke with an American accent; elegant Phyllis Thomas whom he pursued as if she were a Queen; lanky Desmond Palmer; and sexy Lorna Simms.

Our colleagues on the Gleaner desks, in the same large open Editorial Department, included Ken Allen, Ben Brody, Carl Wint, Jennifer Ffrench, Cynthia Williams, Dawn Rich and Trevor Fearon.

The Gleaner operated on the hot press system and the printing plant took up the entire third floor just below Editorial. The massive printer went almost to the roof. It was a beautiful thing to see and hear that well-oiled behemoth – the maintenance men had their work cut out for them.

Mr. Clarke, who ran the press room, was the working man's version of Mr. Sealy, very erect and stern. He barely tolerated editors on his floor. Most of his workers being men and most of the sub-Editors being young women, we were a big distraction. Luckily his deputy, Mr. Hector Lodge, was much more approachable.

My job as a copy editor was to prepare the pages I was assigned, making sure the copy was grammatically correct and had an appealing headline. I'd lay out my page in pencil, showing where I wanted each story placed. Then we'd send it downstairs via a copy boy to Mr. Clarke, who distributed them to his linotype operators.

These gentlemen typed the copy on their machines, which transformed it into lines of hot metal. The metal would be moved in huge trays to a layout table where the copy editor was allowed to look on to avoid errors, such as lines being put in the wrong place, as sometimes happened. We were supposed to be able to judge how much space a story would require, but I often got it wrong. Sometimes that required redoing the entire page, which did not endear me to Mr. Clarke.

The company cafeteria was on the fourth floor with Editorial, and everyone from the entire building met in that cafeteria and ate together. It was very egalitarian, and the conversations were very spirited, especially if they involved our political stalwarts such as Ben Brody and Ken Allen. The food was great – including oxtails and rice and peas, curry goat and curry chicken – and affordably priced.

Once Lorna and I were eating together when a stranger came and joined us. With no conversation he wolfed down his food. When his plate was clean, he finally looked up at us and said, "That was the worst meal I ever had!"

We burst out laughing, "We sure couldn't tell!"

Several prominent male reporters at the Gleaner had expense accounts, but I never knew of any women that did. Demure Barbara Gayle, a court reporter, and passionate General Reporter Jennifer didn't have expense accounts, so we girls did the next best thing. The guys did not need much persuasion to take us to lunch.

Positioned at the corner of North and East Street we had access to many amenities, such as the botanical garden where Cynthia and I would go to take pictures at lunchtime, but the best asset of all was the restaurant directly across North Street. A group of guys and girls would go in and the guys would tell us stories about what they were working on, and the conversation would be interesting and very spirited. But once our meals arrived, you'd hear little other than the clink of utensils.

Audrey, and her friend Rhemalee Simpson and I, rented a three-bedroom house at 27 Southern Cross Drive in Harbor View from Mr. and Mrs. Mitchell who lived right next door. He was an entrepreneur and she was a nurse. They had two children, Heather and Michael, and the Mitchells treated us like family. Across the street lived our friend Miriam from Cuba, who we considered a bit eccentric because every single morning she came out and scrubbed down her steps and her gate posts. She was the only person we ever saw do that.

Our street ended at the foot of the hills and the neighborhood was very serene. Practically everyone knew everyone else. After Audrey moved to Canada, Desmond moved in with Rhema and me. Then Rhema married Tom Fearon, my classmate Grandlin's cousin, and moved to Clarendon. Grandlin had taken me to Denbigh to meet the Fearons while we were still at Clarendon College. Tom's mom and dad, Aunt Noon and Mr. Fearon, had 14 children of their own, but took in any child that needed help. They took me into their family as if I was born into it, and I spent many happy days in that boisterous, fun home.

Two years in a row I was chosen to travel around the country as part of the Gleaner's Spelling Bee team with luminaries Hartley Neita and John Akar from Sierra Leone. Mr. Neita was portly and vigorous, where Mr. Akar was sleek and elegant like a Black James Bond. He was rumored to be with the CIA, though no one knew for sure.

Mr. Neita was our Driver, and we drove around the entire island for a week conducting the Spelling Bee in various parishes, after which the winners would go on to the Finals. Naturally, being part of the prestigious Gleaner team, we stayed in fine guest houses that had a restaurant and bar on beautiful grounds. One night I told a Bartender I wanted to try every drink on the shelf, and my travel companions looked at me indulgently. By the third drink I was ready to slide off my chair, and by the end of our first trip I was firmly in the grip of the travel bug.

So when my young English colleague Ian at the Gleaner suggested we go to Cinchona, the Botanical Gardens across from the Blue Mountains, I was only too happy to say yes! He was an adventurer and had his own Volkswagen Bug. We drove up impossibly winding mountains along precipitous drop-offs, and emerged at the top of the mountain in a forest of eucalyptus trees. The air was fresh and the greenery abundant.

I expected it to be like Hope Gardens, our country's jewel in Kingston that we often visited on Sundays. Those lavish grounds were stately and well-manicured, where Cinchona was more wild and unkempt. We could see the Blue Mountain peaks across the valley, and after exploring the gardens we went to sleep in a rustic cabin.

Next day we drove back down the mountain and I carried that feeling of wild splendor with me. I was so happy to know that it would always be there and I could always go back to it.

I was dating a guy named Al, who treated me like a queen until I became pregnant, at which point he disappeared. I was 19 years old and gainfully employed, so I was ready for my baby. My mom was living in the States and my grandmother was very accepting. All my girlfriends were excited that they were going to have a baby niece or nephew.

At work, Mr. Davis tried to treat me like a second-class citizen. I think he wanted me to be fired because of the "disgrace" of being an unwed mother. But Mr. Anderson and Mr. Sealy would have none of it. Passing behind my chair one day, Mr. Sealy said loud enough for him to hear, "When you have the baby, you can bring the crib and put it right behind your desk."

I gave birth to an exquisite, six-and-three-quarter pound girl, Lisa Nicole Martin, on October 23, 1971. I was able to afford a helper to care for her while I went to work and later I took her to live with Mama in the country. I went back every weekend to visit, determined that I was going to have a closer relationship with my daughter than my mom had with me.

Mama died suddenly when Lisa was just two years old. I was going back to the country every weekend, but the previous week I'd told her that I was going to skip a week. I found that I couldn't stay away.

When I changed transportation in May Pen I ran into Evelyn Bloomfield who was very surprised to see me.

"How did you get here so fast? Did you get the telegram already?" she asked.

"What telegram?" I asked blankly.

"I sent you a telegram to let you know that Miss Ida took sick and went into the hospital. She told me you weren't planning to come this weekend."

I went straight to the hospital where Mama, who'd never had a sick day in her life, was lying prone. She was surprised to see me and very relieved, as she'd left Lisa with our cousins. The doctor said she had a ruptured appendix. They were giving her medication and would operate next day.

I told Mama I was going back to Kingston to get more clothes and come back and stay with her. She was concerned that I'd be missing work and I told her I'd get time off for an emergency. When I left she called after me, "God bless you Ruby."

I went to Brother Reggies's house where his wife Henrietta – we called her Miss Thomas – was taking care of Lisa. I told them I'd be back early the next day.

Next morning I arrived at Mama's ward, but her bed was empty. I thought she might have gone to surgery but when I asked a nurse, she told me to sit down because she had something to tell me. Even then I didn't suspect, so when she opened her mouth and said, "Your grandmother died yesterday, right after you left," I felt like a hole opened up in the universe and swallowed me whole.

Mom came from New York and took care of all the funeral arrangements. The day after Mama's funeral, Brother Reggie's son, my cousin Richard, woke up and told us he had a dream in which he saw Mama and she told him that her shoe hurt because it was too small. That was a shock because we had indeed buried her in shoes that were too small, though no one else knew.

We hadn't thought about needing shoes for her and when we got to the funeral parlor the day of the funeral, they didn't have her size. We got the closest size, reasoning that all we needed was to cover the top of her feet. We had spoken of it to no one.

I interpreted that as another example of communication from beyond the veil, though I was sorry to think of Mama being uncomfortable as we would have done anything for her. I took comfort in the fact that she'd know it wasn't intentional.

I moved Lisa to Harbor View, where Auntie Audrey and Auntie Rhema became her second set of mothers. We hired a helper, who cleaned and cooked and took care of Lisa while we were at work. One day I took Lisa to the Gleaner Company with me and introduced her to Mr. Anderson.

He bent down to shake her hand very formally and asked, "How old are you now?"

"You're three," I prompted Lisa, who seemed a little shy.

"I'm a tree!" she piped up.

We laugh about that to this day.

Some years later another boyfriend suggested we take the bus to Mavis Bank and hike up to Cinchona.

"It's only seven miles from there," he said confidently.

We called in sick to work and took three buses to get as far as Gordon Town. We were standing at the turn-off thumbing a ride, when Mrs. G came driving down the road on her way to work. We couldn't have picked a worse spot. I couldn't avoid being seen. She stopped and I ran over to the car, babbling excuses. But she was gracious and smiled and said, "Have a good time."

This lying thing was not working for me. Every time I told a lie it blew up in my face. I strengthened my resolve to stop lying.

We caught a bus going up to Mavis Bank, got off at the last stop, walked through the neighborhood, across the Yallahs River, and started up the mountains. When we'd gone what felt like five miles I said to him, "I thought you said it was seven miles round trip?"

"Yes, I meant as the crow flies," he responded nonchalantly.

At times a fog rolled over and enveloped the road. When we saw it coming we'd lie down because the road was so narrow and the precipice so close, we could easily tumble over. I made up my mind that, if a car came by, whether it was going up or down, I was going to be in it. But not one car passed us the entire time.

Cinchona is magical but, when we got down from the mountains, my roommates were very worried because I could barely walk. Every muscle in my legs ached and it was torture to move. It took several days for the effects to wear off.

Once there was a big occasion involving the Gleaner and Governor General Sir Clifford Campbell, where the schedule had to be pushed back. I was selected to make our apologies. Sometime later when Mr. Sealy retired and Mr. Oliver Clark became the managing editor, I was chosen to conduct the first interview with him. The headline for the article was "Just Call Me Oliver."

In 1977, I signed up for a Diploma in Mass Communications that the University of the West Indies at Mona was offering for people with a background in Journalism. The luminaries in my class included Melba Hippolyte from Trinidad and Jamaican Norman Hall. Melba had a background in Television, Norman in Marketing and PR, and I had a background in Journalism. We became fast friends and study buddies.

Melba lived on campus and we'd go to Papine Market after class and get rich ripe papayas, bananas, sweetsops and all kinds of fruit, and go back to her apartment to eat and study. But I'd often fall asleep and they'd tease me about it when I woke up – that I only came to eat and sleep. Where had I heard that before? They'd distill what they'd learned and, since I paid keen attention in class and tried to grasp the concepts, I did well in all my classes.

We had Professor Rex Nettleford for Political Science, and a more urbane man never lived. Founder of the National Dance Theater Company, his diction and elocution were so elevated and so masterful, he held me spellbound just by opening his mouth. Years later, when Frank and I got married, I told him that if I was ever upset with him, all he needed to do was use those polysyllabic words like Rex Nettleford and all would be well.

Both Rhema and Audrey had multiple brothers who treated all us girls like sisters. Audrey's brothers lived farther away in Ocho Rios, but Rhema's brother Earl Simpson who was only a few years younger than us and lived more than 30 miles away in May Pen became our chief and most faithful facilitator. Wherever we wanted to go – to the beach, the movies, or for a drive in the country, he made it happen.

Our favorite beach spot was Gunboat Beach on the Airport Road where you could park on the wide swale and wade into the water. Everybody went to that beach and, especially on a Sunday, it was very crowded. A drive-in movie theater and an upscale outdoor restaurant were directly across the highway from our housing development, and sometimes the guys would climb onto our roof and watch the action from a distance.

Our other favorite beach spot was Cable Hut on the road to St. Thomas. This was a developed beach with changing rooms, bathroom facilities and a restaurant. We girls loved to wear our pretty bathing suits and lie out on the beach, but we seldom got into the water and most of us didn't swim.

One day I was floating on an inner tube and having a great time when I decided to jump off and wade back to shore. Surprisingly I felt myself going deep and began flailing. I'd floated much farther from the shore than I realized. Suddenly I felt arms lifting me, and Earl was there carrying me back to shore.

"I was watching you and I realized that you didn't know how far out you'd floated," he said.

He became an engineer and I often tease him that it's his profession as well as his nature, because he's always looking ahead and planning for any eventuality.

CHAPTER FIVE

I was not particularly political, and only occasionally read the international magazines Times and Newsweek, de rigueur for people who considered themselves politically active. A young colleague at the Gleaner once chided me, "You don't get them every week?"

Well, no. My world was very comfortable and, based on my experience, it wasn't man that made it so.

But in the Michael Manley years the country became very politically divided and crime came very close. The Prime Minister's alignment with Cuba rankled the United States so much that the International Monetary Fund called in practically all of Jamaica's debts, so that the majority of what we produced went to interest payments.

Under those conditions things took a downturn. I would leave work in the evenings and walk downtown to take the Jolly Joseph bus to Harbor View. I loved those buses and looked forward to the ride home. If I was lucky and got a window seat, I'd be looking at the Caribbean Sea for much of the way, and on the other side mountains stretched to the horizon, once you passed the cement plant on the left.

The buses were usually crowded and a great place to people watch. Men and women hung onto the iron bars in the middle of the aisles, and young children clung to adult legs. Seated passengers often picked up unresisting youngsters and held them on their lap. Pregnant women were assured of a seat, as anyone they stood over would immediately relinquish their seat.

One evening I ran into a political protest downtown, with people swarming the streets and no buses in service. It was a very dangerous scene as the mob mentality was in full force. People were angry that things had gotten tighter economically and the egalitarianism Manley promised was being thwarted. The Gleaner and Star had covered stories of poor people and criminal elements going to wealthy areas such as Beverly Hills and pointing out which house would be theirs "when the revolution come." Recently a thief had literally cut the finger off a woman downtown to get the ring she was wearing. Things had become very tense.

I hid in a space behind pillars in front of an ornate building, and eventually spotted a man from the Gleaner in the crowd. He helped me get home safely.

But then they killed Mr. Anderson, and I knew it was time to leave my country. The venerable Jack had retired a few years earlier and held court in his favorite bars, his shock of white hair and his booming voice unmistakable in a crowd.

He lived just a few streets away from us in Harbor View. One day two men walked into his house, pushed his wife aside, went into the back room where Mr. Anderson was just getting out of bed upon hearing the commotion, and shot him dead.

I was ready to pack up Lisa and leave then, especially as the restrictions on imports had tightened so much that it was impossible to get basic items such as medicine or even cheese. I didn't want to leave my country, but I had to weigh the fact that, if my child got sick, I might not be able to get medication to protect her health.

And the crime had come too close. We learned later that the criminals had been sent to kill a witness in a court case who lived at the same number on an avenue with practically the same name. They had simply made a mistake and now Mr. Anderson was dead.

Mom had been living in New York since 1970 and had finally gotten her green card or permanent resident papers. She'd filed for me and Lisa so our green cards were already waiting for us. All we had to do was pick them up when we arrived at John F. Kennedy Airport in New York.

I had the option of going to the States at a time when Jamaicans were fleeing the island in droves. Many were running from our tilt toward communism, afraid we'd become the next Cuba. It was the great exodus.

The first time I applied for a U.S. visa I was turned down. There were so many people applying that, if you wanted to have any chance of being seen at the embassy, you had to get in line overnight. The Gleaner and Star published pictures of people bedded down on the sidewalk in lines stretching around the block. I joined one of those overnight lines and eventually got processed, but was told I would not be getting a visa. The reasoning was that, since I had a close family member in the U.S., it would be easy for me not to return home.

I was talking about this challenge at work and John Akar overheard. He made a call and wrote a letter for me to take to the embassy, and that time they gave me a three-month visa. After I went to the States and returned in six weeks, I regularly got visas and Lisa and I went to spend vacation with Mom every year.

June 16, 1978, Lisa and I traveled to Norman Manley Airport with a full retinue of supporters. When someone was going to America it was a big affair, and the airport had a waving gallery where people could stand and wave to their departing relatives and friends. Desmond teased me later that I held up the entire line boarding the plane because I stood in the door and waved so long.

I was leaving the land of my birth where I was completely at one with the land, my culture and my people. A new life as an immigrant waited, as my mother and so many others had found before me.

So long, beloved Jamaica! America, here we come!

Lisa and I arrived at JFK Airport with one single dollar to our name. I didn't have much money anyway, and the Jamaican government had set limits on the amount that Jamaicans leaving on a one-way ticket could take with them. Fortunately it was not an issue for me, as my Mom was at the airport with her longtime friend Winston Dyke to pick us up.

She was living in Spring Valley, a rural community in upstate New York. We moved into the old house she lived in that had been converted to an apartment building, and it even had a gurgling little stream in back. It was like having my gully again, though it was fenced off from the property. We had visited many times before, so it was easy for me and Lisa to fit in. I treated it as if we were only going to be there for a short time before we'd be able to go back home.

In Jamaica, the family Mom worked with as a domestic had helped her get a job at Seprod, a factory where they made cooking oil and soap. In America, she could only find work cleaning houses. She had a regular schedule of clients and Lisa and I went with her on jobs many times. The people she worked with included a fireman who was single and who loved us. She showed me how to clean and leave everything spotless, and we were allowed to eat anything in his fridge. It was the first time I ever had a tuna fish sandwich, and everything he had seemed wonderfully exotic to me.

Mom had a very active religious life and had joined the elegant Grace Conservative Baptist Church in Nanuet, New York. There she met the Khaleah family who took her under their wing. Mrs. Khaleah's mother needed full-time care, so Mom morphed into a personal caretaker for her and was gone from Sunday night to Friday evening.

Lisa and I had the small apartment to ourselves all week. I was 27 and she was seven, and we both rapidly made friends among our neighboring tenants and their children. After the first month it began to sink in that we wouldn't be going back home any time soon. Every time a plane went by I yearned to be on it, winging our way back to Jamaica.

It was hard to get used to the fact that, if you wanted to visit someone, you had to call them on the phone and let them know you were coming. This was truly foreign, as in our freewheeling Jamaican lifestyle it would be unthinkable to have to get permission to visit, even though most of us had phones by then.

Later that year we moved to a bigger apartment closer to town and the greatest joy for me was that the apartment complex backed on to an undeveloped plot of land that was full of tall trees. When Fall came, my mind was completely blown to see the rapturous colors of yellow and pink and gold and brown that the leaves changed into. I'd seen photographs of Fall leaves but I had no idea that such a spectacular scene could be real.

I got a job as an administrative assistant at a company that made computer mother boards. It was only a few miles from home and the Khaleahs gave me an older model car that they were no longer using. I'd started learning to drive on a stick shift in Jamaica so within a short time my friend Eddie taught me to drive an automatic and I got my license. Getting around now was a breeze.

The manager I was hired to work with was also new to the company and did not get there until a couple of weeks after I arrived. I'd made friends among the predominantly White office workers and the predominantly Black assembly plant workers. I had to make announcements on the intercom occasionally and people often came by my office to see the person with "that" accent.

When my boss arrived he seemed none too pleased to meet me, which was a surprise because everyone else treated me as if I was wonderful. One of my new friends, learning I was from Jamaica, told me,

"Oh, you're not Black. You're Jamaican."

"Actually, I'm Black," I said. "If you see me walking down the street you don't see a Jamaican, you see a Black person."

My boss was definitely not enamored of me, and kept making weird statements I found vaguely unsettling. But it never occurred to me that he was being racist until the day he said,

"You and your people should still be in the back of the bus!"

I burst out laughing and said,

"Oh, you think you're superior to me? By virtue of what? Looks? Intelligence? Personality?"

He was quite taken aback and I walked out of the office and went straight to the CEO's office and told his Secretary I needed to speak with him. I'd had several conversations with the CEO by then and he was captivated by my crisp British accent and precise diction.

They called in my boss who stuttered and stumbled and could barely express himself. I mean, I had to clean up this guy's English every time he gave me a document to type. The upshot was that he was roundly chastised and made to adjust his attitude.

A young White man, Jack Kraft, befriended me. He was a musician with several albums to his credit, and he offered to take me and Lisa to Bear Mountain one weekend in the Fall. As much as I glorify nature, I never imagined anything like the expanse of forest in all the shades of gold and brown that I saw that first time. As far as I could see from the hillside for almost 300 degrees was a picture postcard scene in which I was enfolded.

Bear Mountain also had a lovely old inn where we could eat and drink, so the experience satisfied all my senses. For years afterward, I'd plan a trip to Bear Mountain on Memorial Day, and even if there was still snow on the ground I would not be deterred.

That first winter was hilarious. I had never seen snow before, and as soon as the first flakes started coming down I ran outside to touch it and feel it and immerse myself in it. I was enthusiastically helping my girlfriend clean the snow off her car when she burst out laughing.

"What's so funny?" I asked.

"Nothing," she gurgled. "Just the fact that I'm cleaning snow off my car with a woman from Jamaica."

But winters were hard for me. I felt burdened by the amount of clothes I had to put on just to go out the door and I didn't like having to spend so much time inside. As soon as March 1 arrived, I would declare winter over, put away my boots and coat, and dress in open-toed shoes. I sometimes caught a cold because I wasn't properly dressed. But I just could not stand the constriction.

At the end of my first winter, I took the bus from Spring Valley to 42nd Street Port Authority and went sightseeing. I was wearing open-toed high-heeled shoes while there was still snow on the ground, and craning my neck looking up and around at all the magnificent buildings. I was in New York City! The fact that nobody called a facility and had me committed is a testament to New Yorker's tolerance for the odd, because the looks I got told me I was definitely not fitting in.

One of the friends I made on the job was Jamaican, and her husband, also Jamaican, was a Supervisor at a company that repaired jet engine parts. When he told me how much money people made in the factory and it was almost twice as much as I was making in the office, I asked him to help me get a job. In a short while that was accomplished, and I started on the late shift working overnight. Yikes!

Thankfully, one of Lisa's classmates, Keisha McCray, lived in the apartment next door. Her mom Doris and I worked out an arrangement that Lisa would sleep at their place at night and I would take care of the girls when they got home from school.

I can't say I was a very good mother in that period, because I was perpetually tired. I'd put Lisa and Keisha on the school bus in the morning when I got home and go to sleep as soon as they left. Then I'd wake up around 2:30 and prepare dinner before going right back to sleep ahead of my 9 p.m. shift. I never felt rested. I truly came to appreciate the value of a good night's sleep and those early morning Zs.

CHAPTER SIX

I learned the job of inspecting jet engine parts and gave it my best effort. It was a big responsibility because, if a part failed in flight, the plane couldn't just pull over at a gas station and get it fixed. I wondered about the safety of flying when someone like me was allowed to be an Inspector, and it was reassuring to know that the parts went through many other finishing processes, including X-rays, that would show any cracks.

I was something of a novelty in the factory where the workforce was primarily male except for a few women in the Inspection Department where I worked. I tended to dress and speak differently from the majority of people, and the managers often stopped by my desk to chat. I had a couple of close girlfriends, one of whom was Jamaican but had lived mostly in England, and a young White woman named Jill.

Jill invited me and Lisa to her home in the hills overlooking the Tappan Zee Bridge, and for the July 4th Independence Day festivities we climbed up on her roof so we could have a panoramic view of fireworks all along the Hudson River. She took us to her family's home in the Hamptons and we spent time with her grandmother in Sag Harbor before going on to Montauk Point, very wealthy areas.

I was captivated by the beauty of the landscape full of unusual flowers such as pink and yellow snapdragons. At Montauk Point we basked in the power of the Atlantic thundering onto the shore.

On my lunch hour one day, I drove home to pick up something and, on the way back, driving down the New York State Thruway, I hit a deer. I was driving in the far right lane with the Nanuet Mall on my right when I saw the animal bound onto the highway. I was still processing that when another one bounded onto the road and I hit it broadside.

The crack when the car hit the deer on its flank, the hood crumpling on my car and flying up to hit my windshield – I registered all of these things as if in a daze. I didn't stop. I just kept my hands glued to the steering wheel for the next 10 minutes until I pulled into the parking lot at work.

Walking in through the office to get to my station in the factory, the executive secretary Marie Fabry caught the look on my face and said,

"What's wrong? You look like you just saw a ghost!"

"Worse," I said. "I just hit a deer on the Thruway!"

Marie and I had only nodded and said hello before then, but after that we became fast friends. We'd go to lunch together sitting out on the lawn in front of the building, enjoying being outside. To this day we talk every couple of months.

While I was working I went to school in the evenings at St. Thomas Aquinas College, which was only about a 10-minute drive away. I was older and one of very few Black students. My favorite class of course was English Literature, and the Sister teaching the class was my favorite faculty member.

After our first assignment when students were reporting out, she said when it came to my turn, "You don't have to say much, just ..."

I got the feeling she was being sympathetic to a perceived inferiority. I wasn't offended because I loved her and I didn't think she was trying to hurt me. But Literature was my favorite subject, people!

When I finished presenting there was a brief silence, as the students and teacher looked at me in amazement. "Now I have to follow that?" the young woman next to me groaned, as the whole class burst into laughter.

In a Social Studies class, the professor asked for a show of hands who was satisfied with their body. My hand shot up. To my surprise it was the only one in the room! I was amazed to find that these gorgeous young people were dissatisfied with their bodies.

How was that even possible? They had every advantage and took for granted things we didn't have when I was growing up in Jamaica – cars, refrigerators, television! Maybe that was the problem. I reasoned that, if a person wasn't satisfied with their body, they should do something about it so they'd be satisfied. Plus, if I sent a message to my body telling it I was dissatisfied with it, how could I expect my body to cooperate with me? That was an eye opener.

Dorrit had married a wonderful young man, Wilfred Nelson, and lived on Long Island, exactly an hour's drive from our door to theirs. On weekends Lisa and I would get into our new Honda Civic and navigate the challenging highway system, across the Tappan Zee Bridge, across the Throgs Neck Bridge and on to the Island.

At first it was terrifying to contemplate and Mom drilled into me that I had to be in the correct lane at all times to make the necessary turn off, because if I missed a turn things could become dicey. I'd have to find my way back to the highway and pick up the trail again. But like most things, once I did it, it became easier each time.

Going to visit Dorrit was like a mini-vacation back to Jamaica. Fred was an excellent cook and always had my favorites ready – ackee and salt fish or oxtails and rice and peas, depending on the time of day. We often drove down for their daughter Shanelle's dance recitals, interspersed with impromptu parties that Dorrit could put on at the drop of a hat. Two of her sisters Millie and Maisie and her brother Clifton lived nearby, so with their families we already had a good number for a party. Their friends became our friends. We'd all go into Manhattan shopping, sightseeing, visiting museums, or to see a play.

Dorrit and Fred both worked on Wall Street and took the subway to work. One Monday I was excited to have the chance to go to work with her. I could hardly believe the subway experience – being underground out of sight of the sun; the crush of people; the noise, and the pace. I realized how lucky I was to have landed in Spring Valley.

As Dorrit navigated the crowd with her regal long stride, I had to run to keep up with her. Arriving at her imposing Wall Street building, she became a magnet as soon as we walked into the lobby. I was shocked at the level of deference all these people were showing my friend.

A young man followed us into the elevator and began telling her quite agitatedly about a significant sum that had been discovered in an account, for which there was no record of a deposit.

"Don't worry. It's probably interest that accrued from trading overseas on the weekend," Dorrit said calmly.

A look of relief came over the young man's face and his whole body relaxed. The rest of the day was more of the same as she took me down onto the trading floor and introduced me to some of the traders.

She told me that once a young White man was telling her how his dad trained him from he was a little child to carry a briefcase and practice how he'd act on Wall Street. He looked at Dorrit and asked her, "Did your father teach you that too?"

The idea made her burst into uproarious laughter because our fathers who were friends, had no idea that there was even such a thing as a place called Wall Street.

I was still looking for work in Communications and answered an ad for a copy editor at Right On! Magazine. I got the position out of many applicants. The magazine focused on the entertainment industry and was an icon among Black Americans. Its sister publication Tiger Beat was geared toward younger people.

The editor was an elegant and very polished young woman named Cynthia Horner and she evidently liked me because she gave me increasing responsibilities. Soon I was interviewing recording and movie Stars on the phone and writing articles about them. Once we threw a big party at Studio 54 and I was given the job of standing outside the door and checking guests' names against a list before they could enter.

The winter of 1984-85 was the worst. One morning I went to my car and found that the tires were frozen on the ice. I had the bright idea that I could go upstairs and get the kettle of hot water and pour it under the wheels. Hey presto! The ice would loosen its grip and I'd be off to work.

It didn't turn out that way. The ice only became slick and I almost busted my rear when I slipped on it.

Another time I was driving to work on a very icy road which ran along a precipice that fell down to the railroad tracks. A train was coming and ahead I could see cars sliding all over the road. Before I had a chance to stop I was caught in the slide, and barely managed to bring the car to a halt before it could have tumbled down onto the tracks. That was chilling.

But what took the cake was the Friday I was leaving work and the radio announcer said the temperature would fall below zero that weekend. I hadn't experienced below zero before, so I made sure we had enough food in our apartment and I didn't have to go out over the weekend.

Monday morning I started the car and pulled down the handbrake, but the brake light stayed on. There was a garage about a block away, so I drove the car there and the owner told me the brake cable was frozen and I needed to leave it inside for a while to thaw out.

I thanked him and decided to walk back to my complex to my friend Albertine Phipps' apartment and ask her to drive me to work. Miss Phipps and Mom had been friends since they were young women in Jamaica, and her son Ernie Nelson and I were like brother and sister. As I was running, my eyes started to water and my nose began to run. I felt the tears freeze on my cheeks as the wind cut through me.

"Oh my God!" I thought. "Surely You did not intend for people to live like this?"

When I got to her apartment, the thermostat must have been near 80. The apartment was so toasty, compared to the icebox I'd just come out of. Her TV was on Channel 10 ABC and weatherman Spencer Christian was in the act of saying, "And in Fort Lauderdale today the temperature is 78 degrees . . ."

I didn't need to hear anymore.

"That's where I'm going to be next year," I declared.

"You're going to leave your good-paying job and move to Florida? You know that wages are very low in Florida, right?" Miss Phipps said.

"No, and I don't care," I responded. "I'm not going through this another year."

A year earlier Mom had married Arthur Golding and they went to Fort Lauderdale for their honeymoon. They came back with huge Julie mangoes that they got from Arthur's brother's house, and said Florida was just like Jamaica with mangoes and coconuts everywhere.

This clinched it. I wanted to live in a place where I didn't have to wait all year for my two week vacation to have fun. I wanted to be able to go to the beach every weekend if I chose, just as I had done in Jamaica. In Fort Lauderdale I'd be able to do that.

CHAPTER SEVEN

By then I was working at IBM in the Selectric Typewriter department. I didn't enjoy it and the only good thing was that my friend Marie also worked there.

Lisa said she wanted to stay with Mom so she could graduate from middle school with her class. Of course I agreed, and the day after my birthday, August 22, 1985 I got into the car with my boyfriend Jimmy for the drive.

It was 1300 miles to Fort Lauderdale and we decided to do it in two days. We stopped in Santee, South Carolina, and I heard the Southern accent for the first time. It sounded as funny to me as my accent must have sounded to the people on my job in New York. I was about to comment on it to the receptionist at the hotel we stayed when I saw Jimmy glaring at me as in, "Don't say it. They won't appreciate it." So I kept it to myself and just enjoyed the culture shock.

Arthur's brother had helped me find a three-bedroom house just around the corner from him, and I was ecstatic when I got there and found it had mango trees and sugarcane in the back, as well as a lovely flower garden with crotons in front. Just like Jamaica! Wow!

Our plan was that Jimmy would help me drive down and get settled, and then he'd fly back home to New York. Fortunately he had a friend from New York named Grace who lived in Plantation, a suburb of Fort Lauderdale, with her adult daughter. They had a Public Relations business and she introduced me to the publisher of the Westside Gazette, a newspaper founded by Levi Henry Jr. that was focused on reporting positive news about Black Americans.

Grace was very popular and would take up her station at the local watering hole, a bar near the intersection of Interstate 95 aptly named I-95. Everybody who was anybody went there. I was happy to tag along and when I was introduced as a friend from New York, people must have thought I was hip.

I was having a drink with a young attorney when he said to me,

"I'm going round the corner and get some coke."

"Why don't you just order it from the bartender?" I asked.

The look he gave me! Grace couldn't stop laughing when I told her later that night and she informed me what he really meant. I can only imagine the look on my face!

Within a month Lisa had had enough and decided she was ready to come home, which made me very happy. It was a little lonely and isolated in suburbia on my own. I was beginning to think the house and land were too much for just the two of us. Then one morning I stepped off the verandah and was about to step onto the driveway when a big black snake uncurled itself from right where I'd been about to put my foot, and slithered into the garden.

Game over! The same day I called my landlord and told him I was planning to move. He didn't like it and he had the upper hand since I'd signed a lease. But when he heard my distress and determination he reluctantly agreed. Within the month I found a two-bedroom apartment for rent at Glen Cove in Lauderdale Lakes and we moved in.

What a difference location makes! Where we had been isolated before, now we had a neighbor Janice with a daughter who was Lisa's age, and on the ground floor Jamaican Angela who was about my age had a son that went to the same high school. On top of that, the complex had a pool where residents hung out, so it was easy to make friends.

I was having trouble finding work and was living off my $5,000 Dreyfuss investment account that Dorrit had encouraged me to get. I went on a few interviews wearing my power suit, a black skirt with a white jacket that ended in a triangle highlighted with a black stripe along the edges and buttoned on the side.

The children laughed whenever they saw me in that suit because they knew it meant I was on the job hunt. But the wages people were offering! They were so low that I reasoned I was better off without a job so I could spend my time looking for one that offered a living wage.

Many times I gave up and took the kids to the beach instead. But funds were getting perilously low. One Saturday morning I woke up with one chicken in the freezer and $100 to my name, and no prospects. I called Dorrit and, in the process of telling her my situation, I broke down crying.

"Don't worry," she reassured me. "Everything will work out."

And she sent me $100. That investment restored my joie de vivre. My main concern was that teenage Lisa should not feel deprived, and it was the ultimate relief for me when some years later she asked innocently,

"Mommy, did we ever have any money worries when we lived at Glen Cove?"

I laughed out loud with joy. She hadn't even known, and I was happy because I really wanted her to have the carefree childhood that I had.

I wrote feature stories for the Westside Gazette as a Freelancer and, after just a few months, Publisher Levi Henry and his wife Yvonne called me in and told me that he'd been invited on a press trip to Germany and he wouldn't be able to make it. They asked if I wanted to go in his place with the group of Black publishers from all over the South.

Of course I jumped at the chance, and Janice agreed to look out for Lisa for the week we'd be gone. Jimmy was not impressed when I told him, arguing that I had not yet found a real job and it was irresponsible to be going off on a jaunt. I dismissed his objections.

It was my first trip to Europe, and how fortunate to have an all-expense paid excursion where we were hosted by some of the top leaders in Germany. We visited Frankfurt, Munich, Heidelberg, Bonn and West Berlin. I was most impressed by the natural beauty of the country because, from reading Leon Uris' books about World War II and the Resistance, I'd gotten the idea that it was a barren, dreadful place.

The City of Heidelberg was my favorite, and in Bonn we took a cruise up the Rhine River where I felt I was literally in the pages of a fairy tale, with castles on both sides and more every time we turned a bend. We disembarked and went on a walk through the mountains up to an old tavern where we had hard bread, cheese and beer. It was divine.

We were in Munich for Oktoberfest and joined in a festival featuring beer, sausage, music and men in lederhosen. Very fun. I can hardly remember what any of the talks were about, except for Berlin where we visited the office of a newspaper that was so close to the Berlin Wall that we could look down and see people walking around in communist East Berlin.

When the Gazette was invited to send a reporter on a flight of the Goodyear Blimp, I leapt at the chance. What an incredible experience. The attendants cast off the lines and the huge blimp soared quietly and effortlessly above the treetops and into the sky. I felt as if I had "slipped the surly bonds of Earth" and was floating among the angels. I also had the opportunity to meet and interview astronaut Mae Jemison, a lovely lady who recalled her childhood in Chicago, lying on the rooftop and looking at the stars, dreaming that one day she would be among them. Dream realized!

Eventually I took a job as an administrative assistant at a hotel on Fort Lauderdale beach. The setting on the Atlantic was exquisite and fulfilled my need for nature and beauty, but the pay was so low! I was telling a woman I'd become friends with that I just couldn't live on $7.00 an hour. She smiled smugly and said, "Well, I've been here seven years and I'm making over $9.00." I decided it was time to go.

At my exit interview the very kind people told me all the wonderful things they offered their employees. I suggested they pay a living wage so their employees would want to stay, and departed on amicable terms.

My next foray was with a friend who had a secretarial service that she was trying to market to business people as a way to cut their costs. They would forward their phones to her office and have the benefit of a live person taking the call instead of an answering machine.

I was marketing the opportunity without much luck since wages were so low that people could easily afford to pay someone to be in their office. But the big bonus was that one day FRANK came in. Wow! This guy was so elegant and so debonair, he was the real Black James Bond. He came in to get the manuscript he'd written edited and retyped, and I was massively attracted.

Thankfully, he was equally smitten with me and we became very good friends. He introduced me to his mom Veta Mae and his dad Frank and we all got along great. He was so intelligent and learned and I was desperately in need of a friend with those attributes. He was separated from his second wife pending a divorce. I became his sounding board for the female sex, and he became my sounding board for my dates.

"Why is it that I can make it clear to a woman that I'm not interested in a serious relationship and then she proceeds to demand a serious relationship?" he asked one day.

"Because when you say that, the person hearing it assumes you're talking about other people, not them," I said. "She takes it that she's the exception."

Whenever we didn't have dates on weekends, we'd go out with each other to bars and restaurants and art exhibits and plays. I decided that this guy was so great I was going to fix him up with one of my girlfriends. I didn't want to start a romantic relationship with him, in case it didn't work out and then I might lose my friend.

I introduced him to some of my most beautiful friends, and occasionally even went on dates with them. Often it was a complete disaster. Once I went with him and a young lady to a fancy restaurant on the water. They seemed to dislike each other on sight. They traded barbs the entire evening and I couldn't stop laughing.

"Why do you keep trying to set me up?" he asked after that. "I don't have any difficulty finding a date on my own."

I knew that was true but I didn't stop trying.

The marketing position did not work out because no one really needed that service. I wasn't making any money so I left. I found a job at a family-owned credit counseling service just across the street from my apartment and worked with them for seven years.

By then Mom and I had bought a three-bedroom house just up the street in Lauderdale Lakes. She was still living in New York and provided the down-payment. The house was on a corner lot and had a mature mango tree that produced the biggest mangoes I ever saw. It also had an avocado tree, an ackee tree and a grapefruit tree. Heaven! Mom and I joked that all we needed to do was plant a salt fish tree and we'd have the fixings for our favorite Jamaican dish - ackee and salt fish with avocado - growing in the backyard.

Lisa was able to continue going to the same high school and when the credit counseling office moved about a mile away, I went with them as their longest-serving employee and my title was bumped up to manager.

I had a big office right off the reception area where a beautiful young woman named Cindy Gluck was the receptionist. Frank would sometimes drop by to visit and I'd encourage Cindy and the other girls, "Come, feel his muscles. See how good he feels," and they'd come trooping in to squeeze his biceps. Frank was very much the cock of the walk.

Cindy and I did a lot together, including going to the mall, where she had her own personal shopper at Macy's. I didn't even know there was such a thing as a personal shopper. One day Cindy was confiding that she was very concerned that her romantic relationships didn't last, and I jokingly gave her the old Jamaican saying, "Don't worry. Every hoe got dem stick a bush," which I explained meant there was someone out there for everyone.

"Well, I don't want to wait till I'm 40 to find my stick," she responded tartly.

Thunderclap! Suddenly I realized that I was more than 40 years old and relatively speaking, unattached. I hadn't thought of that before. That evening as I was driving home I said a silent prayer.

"Dear God, if you have anyone in store for me, I think I'm ready now."

Then I put it out of my mind.

CHAPTER EIGHT

One day shortly afterward, Frank told me he went to a party at the home of a Jamaican family and saw a young woman he was attracted to. He said she seemed attracted to him as well, but her partner and the young woman he was with made sure they didn't have a chance to get together. By then he was single again.

"Oh, if you can find the house, we can go there, and I will talk to the family and you can describe the young lady and find out if they know who she is," I offered.

For some reason that never happened. A few months later we were coming back from an art exhibition at a university in Miami, quite disappointed in the quality. I was driving and we were talking about how odd the event was, when Frank suddenly said,

"You know, I think we have the makings for much more than a platonic relationship."

"Huh? Where did that come from?"

I turned to look at him and saw that his chin was trembling.

What?! Mr. Suave was emotional?

I realized he was serious. So we made a date to go on a real date. Suffice it to say, that same week we moved in together. I was madly in love with the guy the whole time I was trying to fix him up with other women, and didn't even know it!

Frank was very health-conscious and loved to walk four or five miles in the early morning, several times a week. I was happy to join him and found it the best time to talk and notice things around us - the flowers, the birds, all of nature.

One morning when we were out he said, "Oh, that's a Red-tailed Hawk calling!"

Huh? I love birds but I hardly knew one from another, and this guy could tell what a bird was by the sound it made? If I wasn't already hooked, that would have clinched it. It turns out he can actually call birds down from the trees by making a particular sound. Wow!

Soon we were planning to get married. Frank thought we should just go to the beach and make a pledge to each other, but I wanted a real wedding where my Mom and Lisa and our friends could come. Frank had been married twice before and he had no objection.

I invited his oldest daughter Regina Thompson over to help me plan the wedding. We were in the Florida sunroom sitting on comfy overstuffed couches while Frank, a gourmet cook, chimed in from the kitchen where he was making dinner.

My idea was to have the wedding in Dorrit's friend Alvin's nightclub in New York. Regina was in the process of telling me all the things that would need to happen. By the time she got to the corsages that we'd need for his Mom and mine, I fell asleep. And that was the end of the wedding planning.

A few weeks later we went to the office of Frank's buddy and former law partner Bob Gilligan and he performed the ceremony. His law clerk was our witness. We were ecstatic. We left the office and went straight to Frank's favorite bar at the Sheraton Hotel in Dania to celebrate.

The bar was crowded, but Frank was a regular - I used to tease him that he should have his name carved on a stool there. The bartender told a White couple seated at the end of the bar, "Get up! That's this man's seat," and they laughed and moved.

I was so shocked. I told Frank he better never say anything like that to me. But apparently the bartender, Jack, had a reputation and it was all part of the fun.

Next we drove to Frank's mom Veta's house just around the corner to tell her the news. Dad had passed on a few years earlier and Mom, in her late 70s, was living in the same house on the lake that they'd bought in the 50s.

She was ecstatic. A classy lady who made her own clothes mostly out of African fabric, covered her shoes with the same material and made her own hat, she and I hit it off from day one. I loved her so much and she loved me.

She gave us some of her famous sweet potato pie with vanilla ice cream. There was never a time when Mom did not have a few sweet potato pies in the freezer that she could just pop into the oven.

When we left her house we were happy and sated. As we drove home Frank exulted, "Oh Honey! The places we shall go and the things we shall do!"

I had no idea what that meant, but everything we'd done until then was fresh and exciting. I was down for the ride.

Shortly afterwards he saw a fare to England on Virgin Airlines, for only a few hundred dollars. It was too good to resist. He suggested we take advantage of it and go to visit England, France and his cousin William "Braddie" Ward in Holland. I'm always ready for a trip, so it was on.

We arrived at Gatwick Airport and took the Hovercraft overnight to the Hook of Holland. When we arrived at the seaport I took one look at the people in the lobby and said to Frank,

"There's Braddie!"

He was astonished. I'd never met Braddie. And sure enough, it was him that I pointed out.

"How did you know?" Frank stuttered.

"He's the only Black man in the crowd!" I said.

We laughed uproariously.

Frank was a few years older than Braddie and they'd spent considerable time together when Frank went to Abbeville, Alabama for summer holidays. When Frank went to Morehouse College in Atlanta, Braddie followed a few years later.

He was a gifted musician and at age 17 was awarded a scholarship to study music in Italy. He said when he arrived and found himself treated as a MAN and not as a second-class citizen, which had been his experience in the land of his birth, he decided he was never going back home. This did not please his father, the principal of the local technical school. He was on the verge of asking the government to intervene as Braddie was still a minor. Braddie convinced his dad, veteran Bill Ward after whom he was named, to let him stay. Once he turned 18, he knew his dad couldn't force him to go back to the States.

When his funds ran out he joined with some other Americans he met in Rome and formed a gospel band to sustain himself. Then he married an Italian woman and they moved to Australia. After they divorced he met Marion, a young woman from Holland, and they got married and moved back there to be near her ailing mother.

As time passed, Braddie became more convinced than ever that he would never come back to America and subject his White wife and mixed-race sons to the indignities that he thought would be inevitable. When his war veteran brother died and he felt compelled to return home for the funeral, he steeled himself. Imagine his amazement at the changes in the society he'd left in the 60s when he returned in the 1980s!

"When I walked into the bank and saw a Black girl behind the counter, I almost fell over," he laughed.

What a great reunion we had! Braddie took us home to Marion and their sons Daniel and Alex. They lived in a high rise overlooking the Waterweg. Marion did the laundry at night, explaining that there was less demand on the power grid. Then she hung the clothes out to dry, a conscious choice to reduce their use of electricity.

Frank and Braddie were sitting on the balcony, having a drink and catching up, when I heard him exclaim, "What the?"

And Braddie burst out laughing.

Because there, riding high above us, a ship was going by!

Frank looked at his drink as if he was suddenly seeing pink elephants. Braddie explained that, because much of Holland is below sea level, the dike system they developed allows the water to be raised or lowered, thus allowing the ship to appear to be passing above us.

It was 1992 and the Dutch were already bringing cloth bags to the grocery store, as the government required them to pay for plastic bags as a means of discouraging their use.

Braddie worked as a lounge singer in some of the largest hotels. The whole family went for dinner at the hotel he was working, and we were plied with drinks from the other customers once he announced we were his cousins visiting from America.

Then unfolded one of the funniest scenes ever. A little blonde girl already dressed in her pajamas got down from her chair, dragged it over to our table, went back and got her storybook, handed it to Frank and climbed back up into her chair. She looked at him and waited expectantly for him to read her a story.

Frank tried his best, but the Dutch words twisted his tongue into all kinds of unappealing sounds. The child looked at him as if to say, "What kind of Grandpa are you that you can't read a story?"

Daniel, 11, and Alex, 9, leaned over the back of Frank's chair trying to help him. The whole restaurant was doubled over in laughter.

The boys spoke English, French, Italian, German and Spanish, and in conversation would slip into whatever word best fit what they were trying to communicate. We often heard Marion pleading, "Boys, please use one language or the other?"

We visited Amsterdam, Antwerp and Belgium and marveled at the buildings and town squares many hundreds of years old. I was able to stand on the border of Holland and Belgium with one foot in each country. After a thoroughly enjoyable visit, we left for Paris where we visited the Louvre, the Arc de Triomphe and the Eiffel Tower, among the other "must see" destinations.

We took the train to Boulogne where we planned to take the Hovercraft back to London. The conductor came into the compartment and asked for passports. Frank handed him his passport, the conductor checked it, handed it back to him and left. But when we got to Boulogne and we were in line to board the Hovercraft, I suddenly found myself separated from Frank. The Immigration Officers shuttled me into a little glass booth and began telling me that I was an illegal alien because I did not have a visa to get into France. They threatened to stamp my passport with a black cross and ban me from ever coming back.

I was totally bemused. We hadn't realized that I needed a visa. Traveling on my Jamaican passport there was no issue getting into England, and Frank with his American passport did not need a visa to get into France, but I did. When the conductor checked his passport on the train he hadn't bothered to check mine, presuming I was American since we were together.

By that time Frank realized that something was wrong. I could see him trying to make his way back to me and the immigration officers telling him he couldn't pass.

For a moment Frank came close to the thing we'd laughed about and vowed not to be, The Ugly American abroad.

"That's my wife. And I'm going to see what's going on with her," he told me he said to them.

They let him through.

When he got up to the officers who were interrogating me, Frank cut through all the talk and went straight to the heart of the matter.

"How much?" he demanded.

The officer told us an amount approximating $40 US. And just like that, we were through.

In London we went into a pub to have a drink and soak up the atmosphere, but the smoke was so thick we went in one door and out another, without so much as a pause. We tried a restaurant where we had fish and chips and steak and kidney pie, and stayed at a bed and breakfast before flying home next morning, thoroughly satisfied with our continental tour.

****

CHAPTER NINE

Soon after we met, before we were married, I'd visited Frank at his house one day and found him building a model of a two-story house out of cardboard. He said he was working out the design of the house he planned to build in Belize.

"Belize?" I blurted. "When are you going to Belize? I'm coming with you! You are not leaving me here!"

"Why would I take you to Belize? That would be like taking coals to New Castle," he said coolly. "There are so many women in Belize, why would I bring a woman I'm not sleeping with?"

Ouch! Well, whatever. I just knew I did not want to be there without him. He was my best bud! We did practically everything together and talked on the phone every day.

I asked why Belize and he said that one night he woke up with the TV watching him and saw a program about Belize. It showed how much the Belizeans love their country and believe that the land is the most important thing they have to leave to their descendants.

He said when they needed to build a highway, they strung ropes across it, so that the wild howler monkeys in the forest would have a way to get to the other side without getting killed. He really admired that ethic and thought it was a place where he'd fit in. His plan was to open a bed and breakfast somewhere in the countryside and get to talk with visitors from all over the world.

So, a little while after we got married, he suggested we take a few weeks off and go check out Belize. We made our plans and, months ahead, went to a travel agency and got our tickets. On Christmas Day 1992 we were ready to go.

On our way to Miami International Airport we stopped by his mom's house and enjoyed a lavish dinner of turkey with stuffing and all the fixings, and topped it off with sweet potato pie.

Arriving at the airport we checked in at TACA Airlines and to our delight, ran into Frank's longtime friend Attorney George Allen and his wife Enid who were also headed to Belize City. Oh joy! But when a flight was called and they got up to board, we realized that it wasn't our flight number. We went to check and found to our astonishment that our tickets that we'd had for months were to San Pedro Sula in Honduras, NOT Belize City.

So that was a quandary. The airline said there was nothing they could do. Frank called his friend Charles Fulwood in New York to tell him the situation and ask his advice. Charles had worked for Amnesty International and traveled the world, but even he did not have any suggestions.

Crestfallen, Frank suggested that we might as well go back to his mother's and have some more of that delicious food. But I was not having it. We planned to go to Belize and I was going to Belize that day. I went back to the counter while Frank waited, convinced I was wasting my time.

When I came back to him waving two tickets to Belize, he could hardly believe it.

"You really are an obeah woman, aren't you?" he joked.

George and Enid couldn't believe it either when they saw us board the plane. Arriving in Belize City, we went immediately to have a cocktail, with plans to meet up again. We didn't spend much time together as they were more interested in the city and we wanted to explore the countryside.

Frank and I fell madly, passionately in love with Belize. No question, we wanted to move there. We went to Guanacaste which I learned later was a national park, and where I heard huge iguanas thrashing through the canopy. We went to the market, which was just like the market in Jamaica, and I picked out fruit and started eating it even before we paid. Frank was captivated by the Belizean women dressed in business attire riding their bicycles to work, and we noticed people casually walking alone at night.

We took the bus to Dangriga where Frank read that the highest number of Black Belizeans live. On the bus we could see why they call themselves the "salt and pepper" nation, because members of the same family ranged from White to ebony. Passengers handed young babies through the window to other people to hold, even before they got on the bus.

The roads were winding and narrow, very similar to Jamaica, and at some points it looked like the bus tires were barely on the road and partially hanging over. At one point the bus stopped to change drivers and we waited for what seemed like an hour for the new driver. We had no issues because we were in no hurry, the countryside was lush, and the people warm and wonderful.

It was December 31, New Year's Eve and, after a wonderful day, we caught the bus back to Belize City. It was very crowded but we found seats near the back where all the luggage was stacked, and I actually had a rooster in a box behind my neck the entire time. It was very funny.

Back at our hotel we turned in and sometime very late we heard boots thundering up the stairs. Then someone banged on our door, hard. In one motion Frank woke up, leapt out of bed and grabbed his big Bowie knife from under the bed and marched to the door.

"WHO IS IT?" he demanded in a harsh voice.

Just as fast as they'd come up, the boots thundered back down the stairs. We'd seen quite a few rough-looking characters around. There was unrest between Belize and neighboring Guatemala, and when we landed on Christmas Day we saw soldiers on the tarmac with automatic weapons. But nobody bothered us, so we reasoned that our visitor may just have had the wrong room.

I told Frank later that his eyes had turned blood red. It was as if he'd been transformed to meet a perceived threat. It certainly increased my sense of security.

Walking down the street our first day in Belize City I was wearing shorts and I noticed I was attracting a lot of attention. In America I was accustomed to men looking at me, but especially if I was with Frank they'd show respect and look away. When I saw the protracted stares I told Frank we should go back to the hotel so I could change, because I realized that if something negative happened I'd be putting him in danger having to defend me.

He always told me, "Honey, if something happens, you run and get help."

I never said yes to that because I couldn't imagine leaving my spouse in trouble. But I was a very fast runner, and he often said,

"I don't worry about my wife because I know she can outrun anybody, even in heels."

One day we took a trip to see the Lamanai Mayan Pyramid. We caught the country bus to the recommended spot, and negotiated with a gentleman who had a small flat-bottomed boat to take us upriver to the pyramid. We always travel with a flask of Courvoisier, and as we were going languidly through the serpentine river I poured Frank a drink and poured one for our new friend.

We saw lots of Caiman crocodiles lounging on the banks, as we meandered past many small islands. When he finally pulled over to the shore, we jumped off the boat directly into the water up to our ankles. Our captain told us he'd be back to get us later and took off.

There was not a soul around. A small dog barked at us, yapping as if to say, "Follow me!" So we followed him into a clearing where we were met by a family of Belizeans, including children. They told us to just follow the dog and he would take us to the pyramid.

WHAT? We actually had a GUIDE dog? It was an amazing experience. As we walked through the dense forest we could hear rain above us in the canopy but it did not penetrate to the ground. Whenever we came to a fork in the trail, the dog would take one road and bark at us vehemently if we tried to take the other, and sure enough he took us straight to the base of the pyramid.

Climbing it was a spiritual experience, as we thought of the people who'd built it and who'd walked up those steps centuries before. We couldn't help noticing how far apart the steps were and were fascinated because the Mayan people were reportedly quite short.

After we'd drunk in the views and absorbed the feeling and energy, we descended to find our guide dog patiently waiting for us. He took us back through the forest to the river. In all the time we'd been on the trail we hadn't seen another soul, and by then the family was nowhere to be seen.

It was approaching dusk when our captain returned, and we happily climbed into the boat. It wasn't long before we realized that he didn't seem to remember the route, and Frank mouthed to me, "He's drunk!" He always told our friends to watch out when I pour them a drink because I pour quite liberally.

Then the gentleman said to us, "Do you have a flashlight?"

Oh boy! Of course we didn't. Thank God our luck held and he finally made it back to the village.

But the adventure was just beginning. The charge was $50 and Frank wanted to give him a nice tip. But we didn't have enough small bills, only $100s. The gentleman took the money and left us to go get change. We could see lights coming on in several houses, and then he came back and told us to come with him. We went to a house where I was surprised to see the people still had a dirt floor, but they were pleasant and welcoming and we eventually got the change worked out.

But now came the real challenge. They told us that the last bus to town had already left and there wouldn't be another one that day. What?! We hadn't thought of that. We'd passed a point in the road where there was a large block standing in the center at what looked like a toll booth. Our captain told us it was intended to slow down traffic. So we climbed up on it in a darkness we had not experienced in years, as there was no electricity in the vicinity.

We could hear animals calling and we even fancied there might be a jaguar or two out there, as they still live in the wild in Belize. We drank the remainder of our cognac and were as happy and content as if we were in our hotel. Whatever happened, we were together and we would make the best of it.

Suddenly, out of the dark night we heard the sound of a vehicle, and lights came hurtling toward us. Frank leapt down and ran as close as he could to the road so he'd be visible, waving like mad. A bus pulled up with a screech and the driver opened the door.

Looking at us in wonder he said,

"You must be the luckiest people in the world! I wasn't planning to go back to town tonight. Something just came up!"

Well, something came up alright because we were saved! Instead of having to bed down on a concrete block, we made it back to our room and our nice comfy bed. I thanked and praised God with a great amount of fervor.

I went back home to the States and Frank stayed on for several more weeks to scout out the country and find a place suited for our dream business. I wanted it to be close enough to the rainforest so I could go to sleep at night with the sound of the howler monkeys in my ears.

But when Frank came home, he had a very different plan.

"Honey, I was in this bar having a beer and talking with a Belizean gentleman. He was telling me how much he enjoys cowboy movies that they get on a channel there, and I told him how I grew up watching cowboy movies in the theatre with Seminole Indians, and what an experience it was as they didn't root for the White heroes.

"Then he asked me what the Badlands look like, because many of the cowboy movies were filmed in the Badlands. When I told him I didn't know and I'd never been to the Badlands, he was puzzled.

"He asked me again if I live in America and I told him yes. Then he asked me what the Grand Canyon looks like. And again I had to tell him I didn't know. You should have seen the look on his face, like he just couldn't understand that.

"Honey, can you imagine being at our bed and breakfast and people asking us questions about our country and we don't know? I would feel very foolish. So how about we take some time off and take a trip around the country and see the sights?"

"What?!!" said the original ride-or-die girl. "Sign me up!"

For the next two and a half years we cut back on our spending and saved as much as we could, as we expected to be gone for up to three months. We sold the house and moved into an apartment. Frank did the research and bought a state-of-the-art Sierra tent that weighed four pounds; sleeping bags rated to keep us warm in weather as low as 32 degrees; a backpack; and various implements and utensils to cook with.

Our biggest and most fun purchase was the F-150 truck we called Big Red. The moment we saw it on the lot at the dealer, we fell in love. On top of everything else it had two gas tanks and, since we were planning to be way out in the middle of nowhere, that was very desirable. I stayed with the truck while Frank went to find a salesman.

When a man came by and showed interest in it I said, "That's already sold," because in my mind there was no question that truck was ours.

The only small issue was that it was a manual transmission and I'd only learned to drive an automatic. Frank said he'd do the driving and I was responsible for keeping our spirits high, our esprit de corps.

The really big challenge was with our family and friends, none of whom could believe we were planning to drive around the entire country and hike and camp in the woods. "The woods" were considered more dangerous than usual for Black Americans because of the ongoing murder trial of O.J. Simpson. The lead detective incriminating him was reportedly a White supremacist who had gone off to take refuge with other White supremacists in Idaho. The news was thrumming with stories of White militia men making camp in the woods and practicing for covert action.

My mom and Frank's mom were both petrified at the thought of us being so far away from them and from civilization. Each one of them said she'd be on her knees praying for us until we returned home. As a concession we bought one of the new cell phones that was just becoming popular and promised to keep in touch.

Our friends were equally askance.

"Don't you have anything else that you want to do? Why do you want to do this?" one young woman asked me.

But we felt that this was the opening of an exciting new chapter in our lives. We packed up the truck and, on a Friday evening in August, took off from Fort Lauderdale on our great adventure. We had made no reservations anywhere, and had no particular time when we needed to be wherever. Frank said we had to see the Grand Canyon, Yellowstone and Yosemite in particular, and I was overjoyed.

"Do you have any idea how many millions of people from all over the world come here every year to see these places, and we live here and we've never seen them?" he asked.

Say no more! I was ready to see the wide, wild world.

****

CHAPTER TEN

Our first challenge came right out the gate. Less than an hour north on the Florida Turnpike we came upon the traffic jam to beat all traffic jams. It was so bad, people were out of their cars and lounging on the swale. We settled down to wait as we had no choice. I assured Frank that all was well.

"We're getting the worst out of the way at the beginning," I encouraged. There's a reason I was in charge of the esprit de corps.

It wasn't until early morning that the traffic started moving again. We drove to Orlando and booked a hotel room, cleaned up and went to the graduation of Frank's daughter Andrea, and then got back in the truck and continued north.

Days later we arrived in New York where we stayed with my mom, and I was happy to show Frank some of the places where I spent the first seven years of my life in America. We visited Dorrit and Fred and Shanelle and my godson Andre at their beautiful home in Yorktown Heights, and Dorrit was the only person who encouraged me to go on the adventure.

"Do what you want to do while you can, girlfriend," she said.

We visited Frank's friend Charles and he asked Frank if he was taking a gun. Frank said no, he didn't plan to. It was a question we'd heard over and over from his male friends. They were concerned that we would run into White people who would not be happy to see us in the woods, and anything might happen.

Both Frank and I responded that we are citizens of the world and we would not make ourselves afraid to do what we wanted. Of course we'd be alert, but we were not going out looking for trouble and we wouldn't arm ourselves. Frank politely declined to take one of several guns that he was offered.

It felt like we cut the umbilical cord. We were on our way to Maine, after which we planned to visit Audrey who was living in Toronto, then continue to Niagara Falls. The countryside was beautiful and ever changing. We decided to stay in motels along the way and set up our tent for the first time at a place where we planned to be for a while.

For days we drove through towns where we didn't see a single human being. The first time we saw a sign warning, "Watch out for moose," I burst out laughing.

"You're certainly not in Kansas anymore, Dorothy," I said.

The state is famous for its lobster industry, and to our surprise when we popped into a McDonald's for breakfast, there was actually lobster on the menu. I wondered who'd buy a McDonald's lobster sandwich when you could get the real thing, fresh, as we got in Jamaica. There were some towns that didn't even have a traffic light, but when we reached Bar Harbor on the Atlantic Ocean I was almost struck dumb by the beauty.

Coming into the town, we saw another Black person for the first time since leaving New York. His back was turned to us, and he was bending over a steaming cauldron outside the Chowder House. Instinctively we wanted to turn back and go talk with him, but we opted to keep going. There was adventure ahead.

Bar Harbor is about as far east as you can get in Maine, right on the shores of the Atlantic. My dominant impression was of neat white buildings spread out along the water and among the greenery of the forest nearby. It gave me such a feeling of calm.

Our destination was Acadia on the edge of town. We read that the area had been the vacation home of the Rockefellers and other wealthy industrialists who had left it to be enjoyed by the public.

The central feature of the park is Cadillac Mountain. A huge stone-faced mountain, its base has a fringe of greenery like a hula skirt. Driving up the mountain I saw that the clouds were suddenly below us, and still the road led upward. When we finally arrived at the top I was sure that I must have died and gone to Heaven, because I couldn't imagine so much beauty on Earth.

As far as I could see into the distance, the water stretched away, dotted with small islands here and there covered in trees. The sun was glinting on the water, making it look like liquid gold. From the other side of the mountain top we could see the Atlantic thundering on to the shore, and gulls wheeled and screamed as they dived for food.

I felt like I'd been living in a mansion and until then I'd only seen the kitchen. Now I'd wandered into the living room and the difference was spectacular.

Standing there in absolute and complete awe, I thought, "Oh my God! The same God that made THIS made me. Just as it is natural and beautiful and perfect, I must be beautiful and perfect too."

I felt infinitesimally small yet gigantic, as if I was connected to everything and everyone. I felt consciously, inseparably connected to God. In that moment I literally fell in love with God and with myself as part of God's creation.

We spent several blissful days exploring and I had my first camping experience. I loved it. I loved being in the woods and sleeping in a tent, going to bed with the stars in my eyes and waking up to the sounds of birds and little animals rustling in the bushes, just like I remembered from sitting by my gully in Jamaica.

In the mornings Frank got up first, started a fire and made us coffee. The smell of coffee and sizzling bacon wafting through the campground was just heavenly.

On our way out of town we saw the Black man again, and this time we made a U-turn into his restaurant. He came toward us beaming and introduced himself as James Raines.

"Any relation to Tim Raines in the Major Leagues?" Frank asked.

"My uncle," James said, smiling. "Why don't you folks come in and I'll cook you a couple of lobsters?"

It was only 11 a.m. but we decided to go for it. We were not disappointed. He put two big fresh-caught lobsters into the pot for us with corn and potatoes, and we had a feast that wound up costing less than $20.

We were full and happy when we said goodbye and took off for Toronto, where we spent a few days with Audrey and her family. They'd visited us in Fort Lauderdale and we were happy to reconnect with her and her husband Scott Yearwood and their children, Celeste and Matthew.

Next stop, Niagara Falls in upstate New York. It was breathtaking and the flow of water impressive. But having just seen the incredible wild power and beauty of Acadia, we didn't feel the same level of awe for something that was mostly engineered. We spent the day and decided to move on, heading for Chicago.

We had been married only three years, and the long truck ride gave us time to talk and get to know each other even better. Early in the marriage Frank had said to me,

"Honey, there's three of us in this marriage. . ."

"Whoa!! I didn't sign up for that!" I interrupted.

"There's three of us in the marriage," he continued unfazed. "There's you, there's me, and there's the relationship. The relationship is made up of how we treat each other, how we speak to each other, whether or not we make each other our priority."

Well that made sense. So we decided that, whatever happened, the two of us would make the decision together, then consider our mothers, our children and our family and close friends, followed by everyone else.

Another time he said, "You know, each of us is going to go crazy sometimes. But it is very important that we don't both go crazy at the same time."

He explained that, if I was upset about something, it would be his job to listen and hear me out, then repeat back to me what he'd heard to make sure he got it right. If he had, he'd explain what had happened to produce that result. If I said he hadn't got the point, we'd start over. I would do the same for him if he was upset.

I felt grateful to be the beneficiary of the wisdom he had learned from two previous marriages. Our blended family included six children and six grandchildren.

Arriving in Chicago, we went to visit Frank's Aunt Eva McKinnon, Veta Mae's sister, and her family. Frank reconnected with cousins that he hadn't seen in many years. I was intrigued that Aunt Eva had an artificial tree in her living room which she called her Joshua Tree. It was her dedicated place to pray.

The male cousins flat out told Frank they thought he was crazy to be going into the woods without a weapon, and brought out a collection for him to choose. Again we said no thanks. We left on a wave of love and headed for the American West.

Our first sight of that cinematic landscape came at the Badlands in South Dakota. We were driving along a highway like any other when we saw the sign for the turnoff to Badlands National Park and took it. The sight that greeted our eyes was so unearthly and stunning that it literally took our breath away. We'd been talking animatedly when we made the turn but now the words dried up on our lips.

Stretching to the horizon in front of us were gigantic pyramids, arches and natural formations made of - EARTH!! It was as if the earth had literally gathered itself up into the giant shapes you associate with the pyramids and temples of Egypt or Central America. Shaped by the wind and rain, they came in hues of purple and orange, red and white.

To say it was jaw-dropping is exactly accurate because when I turned to look at Frank his mouth was literally hanging open in wonder.

"It looks just like the temples at Angkor Wat," he breathed.

Overcome with the beauty and majesty of the place, I felt an extra tinge of pleasure at helping make this dream come true for him. It was the cowboy movies of his youth and the conversation in Belize that had sent us on this journey. Now here we were just a few weeks out and a few thousand miles away, experiencing a completely different world.

Our next big destination was Yellowstone. We drove through the phantasmagoric "Wild Wild West" landscapes stopping at Mount Rushmore with the Presidents' heads carved in stone at the top of the mountain. We passed Devil's Tower, a gigantic rock formation that shot up into the sky, and the place where a monument to Lakota Chief Crazy Horse was just getting started. It was planned to be the largest mountain carving in the world.

When we arrived in Cody, Wyoming, the best accommodation we could find was a tent spot in what had evidently been a horse pasture. There were lots of other people camping in the fields.

The following morning we got up early and went to McDonald's before heading up the mountain. It was very crowded. The day before, we were laughing that we were probably the only

Black people in three neighboring states. As if to prove our point, the teenager serving us was so nervous, we thought it highly possible that we were the first Black people he had ever actually seen.

The drive up the mountain was the most nerve-wracking experience I ever had. There were an incredible number of switchbacks and no guard rails to protect an errant driver from tumbling thousands of feet down the mountainside. I kept having to wipe my hands on my jeans, and I wondered how Frank was managing as he threaded the big truck on that narrow road.

We had long ago established a tacit agreement that in any situation neither of us would ever give way to panic, as that would only place a greater burden on the other. Making the terrifying journey we laughed and talked casually, just as if we were seated on our living room couch.

"You know we have the Blue Mountains in Jamaica," I said. "But now I'm going to have to call them the Blue Hills. Because THIS is a mountain."

Our relief was unspeakable when we got to the top of the mountain and into the park. We began to see herds of giant bison in the fields and some meandered across the roads. All the traffic had to stop and wait until they decided to move. We saw herds of elk, the males bearing huge racks of antlers, and a moose crossed the road in front of us, its gangly legs looking too thin to hold up its big body. I was seeing bison and elk and moose for the first time in my life. What a rush!

We parked in front of the stately Old Faithful Lodge and Frank went to the back of the truck to get out his camera equipment. We'd invested several thousand dollars in a good camera and tripod because we intended to publish stories about our trip.

As we unpacked, a heavyset White man came up to us and introduced himself. He told us he was a reporter from Germany, and that we were the first Black people he'd seen in the park. He wanted to know all about our experiences and we chatted for a bit, but we were in a hurry to get to Old Faithful because we wanted to see it the first time it erupted while we were there.

I'd heard and read of Yellowstone and the famous Old Faithful geyser, and I thought it was the only one. Imagine my surprise to discover that the park is FULL of geysers! A park ranger told us that Yellowstone contains half of all the geysers on Planet Earth.

Arriving at Old Faithful after a short walk from the parking lot, we joined throngs of people sitting on benches waiting for the geyser to go off. When it did, it was the sight of a lifetime.

We heard the rumbling beginning deep in the bowels of the earth, then came a few little spurts, followed by the monstrous eruption of superheated water shooting up more than 15 stories high into the sky. Steam burst from it and a collective whoosh of breath escaped the watchers.

I felt as I had in Acadia all over again - infinitesimally small and yet part of something infinitely grand. The fact that the intervals at which this geyser erupts can be predicted and is never far off, blows my mind. How majestic, mysterious and wonderful is the Earth!

We walked around the geyser field admiring other geysers and especially the Grand Prismatic Spring of deep green ringed with yellow. A park ranger told us that scientists harvesting microbes from that geyser had found some that were proving useful to treat cancer. Wow!

Hours later we walked back to the lodge and went into the Visitor Center. To our amazement our new friend was waiting and came toward us beaming with satisfaction. He was holding our keys, which we'd left in the back of the truck! We thanked him profusely. We didn't even want to imagine what it would take to get a replacement for our keys in Yellowstone.

Later that evening we were standing outside the lodge when Frank looked at a scorched area on the hillside and mused out loud, "I guess that's what burned in the fire of '88...."

"Yes," said an older man standing beside us. "When my father brought me here as a kid they were building that, and when I brought my son they were building that..." he said, pointing.

He told us he was from Chicago and had recently retired and was on a tour of all the national parks. I saw a shadow pass over Frank's face and later I asked him why.

"You know I don't live my life with regret, but when he said that I really felt I missed something by not taking my children to this place. That man and his son have a family tradition here. They feel a sense of ownership of this country. I don't have that, and neither do my children."

"Well, we'll take all our children and grandchildren," I said cheerily.

✳✳✳✳

CHAPTER ELEVEN

We headed out to Washington State where we were looking forward to wading into the Pacific Ocean. Coming into Seattle we were stunned to see what looked like a giant snow cone towering up to the sky, and learned it was Mount Rainier. Wow!! How MUCH wonder is there in the world?

We toured the city and caught the ferry to Port Angeles. Driving off the ferry we were once again deposited into a different world. The sensuous smell of pine trees followed us all along Highway 101, with glints of a river winding its way beyond them.

I did not know that there was actually a rainforest in America but sure enough there was a sign for the Hoh Rainforest. Driving in, I felt this must have been the way the Earth looked a few thousand years ago.

Thick intertwined greenery barely allowed the sun to come through, and it formed dappled patterns on the forest floor. We saw very healthy-looking elk thrashing through the underbrush, and walked the boardwalk trail before heading over to find the campgrounds where we would spend the next few nights.

The Kalaloch campgrounds were in a forest on a bluff directly above the ocean. We pitched our tent and walked down to the beach where we were amazed to see signs warning, "Trees Kill!"

Apparently erosion undercuts some of the huge trees and takes them out to sea, and the waves bring them back to shore with thundering force. An unwary beachgoer could easily get hurt.

We also saw signs telling us that if we encountered a mountain lion we should make ourselves look bigger and make noise to chase it off but, if we saw a bear, we should make ourselves look smaller and back away. We had a good laugh about what might happen if we got the two confused.

The tide was out and we waded into the Pacific Ocean for our first time. We walked about a quarter of a mile out and the water barely came up to our knees. There were tide pools teeming with life that had been left behind by the receding water. We saw scores of starfish, bigger than my hand, in bright pink and yellow, and emerald sea anemones with their tentacles gently sweeping the water. A large crab swam right up to my toes.

It was all I could do not to reach down and touch them, but I was mindful of the admonition not to touch wildlife and not to remove anything from the park. We saw otters playing behind the breakwater and looking at us as curiously as we were looking at them. We took a tour to the Makah Indian Reservation at Neah Bay, eager to soak up the Native culture, but found most of the buildings shuttered and an air of depression hanging over the town.

We decided that Olympic National Park truly deserved the slogan, "A place for the soul to expand and for the mind to be refreshed with the beauty of life."

Having come to the farthest point, it was time to turn around and begin the journey home by a different route. Ahead we had the City of San Francisco, where we planned to reconnect with our friend Monica Campbell who had lived with me briefly in Fort Lauderdale, before driving up to Yosemite. We enjoyed that beautiful city and a great reunion, and once again packed up and took off.

Once we stopped to refuel at a gas station and I heard Frank talking to a Hispanic man who was asking him if I was his wife and how he managed to get me to go camping with him.

"My wife grew up poor and she won't even go in the backyard," he said. "She says it reminds her too much of that hard life."

Frank laughed and said, "I guess I just got lucky, man."

I laughed to myself thinking about the circumstances I come from, though I never heard the word "poor" when I was growing up, nor knew what it implied. I definitely knew that some people were "rich," including my father, but the opposite word was not in our vocabulary.

We arrived in Yosemite Valley at dusk and headed for the lodge. We hadn't made a reservation and assumed that our luck would hold as it had throughout the trip. So we were shocked when the perky young woman behind the desk said, "Sorry, we are completely booked."

She must have seen the stunned look in our eyes because she added, "Oh, don't worry. It's your forest. Just pitch your tent anywhere."

Then, as we made our way out the door, she added, "Remember to hang your food in the trees. There are a lot of bears around!"

OK then! We had really done it now. The nearest town was many miles away. We'd been driving all day and were really looking forward to rest. We drove around, passing several campgrounds where campfires were burning and people were enjoying themselves a little too noisily for us. We did not find a place we wanted to camp and finally decided that we'd just park on the side of the road and spend the night.

It was September 23, the night of our third anniversary and we had food and wine in the back of the truck. The only question was how to get them out, since we were on the edge of the forest where bears might be.

When the hunger pangs started, we decided that Frank would take his machete out from under the seat where he kept it, and we would walk to the back quickly with our head on a swivel. Mission accomplished, we went back to the cab with a loaf of round, crusty bread, some cheese we had in the cooler from Wisconsin, and a bottle of our favorite red wine. We consumed them blissfully while furtively looking through the windshield and the windows, keeping a sharp eye out for bears.

Then of course, wine being a diuretic, we had to make several trips outside to relieve ourselves, one or the other of us holding the machete. What a night! We slept with the key in the ignition in case we needed to make a hasty get away. Periodically one of us would jerk out of our fitful sleep and ask, "You OK?" We were never as glad as when day broke next morning.

Here began another completely new experience, as we saw the valley covered in mist like a giant spider's web. As the sun's rays reached the valley, it lifted the mist up to greet it in what seemed to me like a lover's embrace. It was as if we could see the whole Earth breathing. Wow!!

Now that it was daylight and we could see the valley, I was at a loss for words and just gave in to the experience. My senses were overwhelmed by the gigantic trees and by the sight of Half Dome towering into the sky. How was it possible for there to be so many behemoth creations gathered in one place?

El Capitan on the opposite side of the valley was just a little lower than Half Dome which rose a mile straight up into the sky, and looked no less formidable. We drank in as much of the vast scenery as we could and then headed out for Las Vegas.

At the very top of a mountain road reminiscent of the road up to Yellowstone with no guard rail, we turned a corner and there, in front of my shocked eyes, was a huge deer skittering down the mountainside. It had lost its footing and would end up directly in front of our truck. I didn't see how Frank could possibly stop the big heavy loaded truck in time. But he did. He brought it coasting to an easy stop, missing the deer by inches. The animal looked directly at us and bounded off down the precipice.

I asked Frank, "HOW did you do that?"

"I just had a feeling coming round that corner that something was ahead," he said mildly.

Well thank God for his spidery senses! Maybe *he* was the obeah man!

We continued slowly down the mountain, across the Mojave Desert and spent the night in glittering Las Vegas. Next morning we started the drive into Utah, where we planned to visit Zion Canyon. The name alone was magic for me, bringing back memories of all those songs we sang in Sunday School that had Zion as a place where God's power and beauty reigned. It surpassed my wildest dreams.

The hour and a half drive from Las Vegas made me understand in a visceral way why Math and Science are essential subjects, because I could not imagine the calculations engineers had to make to build roads through those huge granite mountains. We went past golden buttes and endless vistas of shimmering mountains until we arrived in Springdale, Utah.

We got a campsite in Watchman Campground on the banks of the Virgin River for $8 per night, and set up our tent. Frank had a hard time driving in the tent stakes because the ground was packed so tight.

"You can almost feel the energy rising up from the earth," he grunted.

Once we got the tent up we went exploring. We saw herds of mule deer feeding in the campground and along the river. The combination of rushing water and large wild animals roaming free, sheltered among the towering cliffs, was mind-blowing. Afternoon passed into evening and then came the most dramatic sunset we'd ever seen. The sun passed over the western cliffs and just like that it was night. The cliffs completely blocked out the sun.

We went to bed watching the stars through the flap of our tent, feeling gloriously satisfied with ourselves. We had been on the road for six weeks and we had seen things that defied even our vivid imagination. I was irrevocably in love with the Earth and the natural processes that guided it year after year after millions of years. To me there could be no clearer sign of God than the creation we saw as God's reflection.

Next morning we watched the sun make its sudden leap over the eastern cliffs, instantly transforming them into vivid colors. We were so eager to see what was inside the park that we didn't even wait to make breakfast.

Driving the scenic highway, our eyes were drawn up to the hills, literally and figuratively, because the monolithic cliff faces, each looking like a huge sculpture, bore Biblical names such as "The Court of the Patriarchs: Isaac, Abraham and Jacob;" "The Great White Throne;" and "Angels Landing."

Our dreamlike state was interrupted by the sight of a young White woman at the side of the road thumbing a ride. Frank and I looked at each other, momentarily uncertain what to do. Would she appreciate two Black Good Samaritans? Without hesitation we pulled over.

She hopped up into the truck as if it was the most natural thing in the world, although we couldn't remember the last time we'd seen any other Black people.

"Thanks for stopping," she said cheerfully. "I'm meeting my boyfriend at a trailhead down the road. We're going camping in the backcountry so he unloaded our gear and I came to park the car. Where are you folks from?"

"Florida," we said in unison.

"I've never been to the South," she said.

She was a California girl and said Zion was her favorite place to get away and relax. We talked all the way till we dropped her off a few minutes later with good luck wishes all around.

Frank and I turned to each other in amazement. If we'd been home watching TV, we couldn't have had an experience like that, and on TV it certainly would have turned out differently.

We spent several days exploring the park, hiking to the top of the cliffs and talking with fellow travelers. When we packed up and left, we were in a heightened state of excitement because our next stop was the North Rim of the Grand Canyon, one of the Seven Natural Wonders of the World, and we were *driving* to see it. We marveled about the experience of traveling across and around the country, experiencing the different topography, the mind-boggling views – all that we would not have experienced if we had flown from city to city.

How could the same country, whose streets we traverse every day, also have places that looked like the Badlands, or Yellowstone, where the earth in some places was no thicker than a potato chip? And how could that fragile place be home to some of the largest mammals on Earth? How could a place like Zion exist, that we couldn't even have conceived of in our wildest dreams? And still the best was yet to come, because the Grand Canyon was the mother lode, the greatest of them all.

For many miles we could see the towering bulk of Zion's cliffs behind us. It was approximately 125 miles to the North Rim of the Grand Canyon, which our map showed was 69 miles from the nearest town. We planned to stay in nearby campgrounds, but when we got there toward dusk, the "Campground Full" sign was up.

We drove the few miles farther to the rim, and our hearts fell when we saw how crowded the parking lot was. There were tour buses disgorging people and not a parking spot to be found. Frank felt it would be impossible to get a room with that throng, and suggested that we start back down the mountain before it got dark.

But I was not hearing it. We were at the Grand Canyon and I was planning to stay. Frank remained in the truck and kept circling while I walked into the lodge, where people were standing three deep at the desk. I heard the clerk tell the two people ahead of me that they had no rooms, and still I stood there.

When I got to the counter he excused himself to take a phone call and came back with a look of amazement on his face.

"You must be the luckiest person in the world," he said. "They just told me on the phone that we have one room open because a guest fell ill and they had to airlift him out of the park."

When I paid the $50 tab and walked out to the truck dangling the key, Frank was in shock.

"I told you you're an obeah woman," he said.

We parked in front of our cabin and went to the closest place we could see the canyon. I'd seen pictures, but the reality was so much different, because the canyon plunged a mile down and spread over innumerable acres to seeming infinity. A panorama of jagged chasms and cathedral-like shapes in every color of the rainbow overwhelmed our disbelieving eyes. It was as if our eyes and mind together could not process so much beauty.

We were amazed to find that we could get some astonishing views just by walking along the rim, but we chose to hike down the Bright Angel Trail so we could appreciate what it felt like below. It was a truly spiritual experience for both of us.

"If colors were music, the Grand Canyon would outshine Handel's Messiah," Frank mused.

We went for dinner in the Grand Canyon Lodge Dining Room. It hung out over the canyon and when the sun went down, looking out the window we felt as if we were hanging out into nothingness.

Following a superb meal, with wine for me and a martini for Frank, we walked back to our cabin feeling like we had been catapulted into Heaven. Looking up at the stars, we saw the Milky Way Galaxy splashed out like a river of jewels in the sky. It felt as if we could reach up and pluck our very own star.

When we finally tore ourselves away from the canyon and made our way back home driving through New Mexico, Texas, Louisiana and Alabama, Frank told our sons and our son-in-law that, if they ever got in trouble with their wives, they should take them to the Grand Canyon.

"If that doesn't work for you, man you've had it," he joked.

Our grand tour of America had covered 40 states and more than 12,500 miles. I felt that, even more than the physical distance, we had traveled a vast distance in our mind and spirit. I saw the Earth and my adopted country in a completely different light. I knew that yes, I am a citizen of a world created by One that loves beauty, variety, harmony and me. I had found the ultimate love.

****

CHAPTER TWELVE

It was impossible to go back to our regular lives. Frank likened it to the old saying, "It's hard to get the boys back on the farm once they've seen gay Paree."

Truly, once I saw the world beyond the cities, I could not rest until everyone else had seen it too. I'd lived in the U.S. for 17 years already. I was a relatively educated and well-read person, and yet I never dreamed that places like that existed, that they were in the U.S., and that I could drive to them so easily and inexpensively. The entire two-month trip had cost us just a little over $3,000.

Inspiration had seeped into my soul. I had seen creation untouched by human hands, the animals and the plants coexisting in harmony as they had since the beginning of time.

Suddenly our way of life felt very artificial. Frank and I'd made gourmet meals in campgrounds – I'd whip up some jasmine rice on the little hibachi we placed on our tailgate while Frank made steaks on the campground grill. A fresh salad or frozen veggies made an easy complement, and we always had a bottle of wine and some cognac handy.

Being so self-sufficient with so few of the trappings of domestic life made me wonder – why do we have so many things? I love civilization, and I was grateful to get out of the woods on weekends when it got crowded and go to a hotel where I could have a hot shower, a comfortable bed, indoor bathroom and food prepared by others. I love the convenience of urban life where I can walk to the supermarket, the bank, the post office, and the theater.

But after seeing what our country looked like before we "developed" it, everywhere I went now I wondered what it looked like before. Worse, I saw with new eyes the homeless and hopeless people packed into concrete enclaves where it was rare to see a tree or any greenery.

Remembering my carefree childhood on my gully bank and roaming the woods in Jamaica, I felt for the children growing up in the "concrete jungle" that my countryman Bob Marley sang about. How would their soul be stirred to create beauty when they were kept apart from the beauty and freedom of wild nature?

The distinction between the natural and the man-made was suddenly hugely apparent to me. It almost physically hurt me to see how much we respect human creations while trashing the creations of God. The sight of the elegant Great Heron fishing in a canal full of trash gave me a pang – man desecrates the world and all the rest of life is forced to live in filth as a result.

Now when I had reason to go into an imposing federal or other building, I kept my sunny personality on display, saying hello and smiling sweetly at people who had taken on the demeanor of "respect" for where they were. No, what I would respect was human beings of all stripes, and all of God's creation. I would walk lightly upon the Earth. Seriously, sometimes I had to remind myself that it was OK to walk on the grass.

I saw God everywhere and in everything. The epiphany I had on Cadillac Mountain stayed with me. I was no better and no worse than anyone, and neither was anyone better or worse than me. I treated the man in the gutter with the same regard that I treated an icon.

Suddenly a conversation that Frank and I had early in our friendship came back to me with increased poignancy. He'd taken me to lunch and during the conversation asked, "Between the President and a man in the gutter, who is more important?"

"The President, of course," I responded.

"Why?" he asked.

"Huh? Because the President can do so much more for society than the man in the gutter," I sputtered.

"Well, think of it this way," he said. "Every human being is worth exactly the same in the sight of God. There is no lesser and no greater human being."

Of course! That's how I live, but I hadn't thought about it that way. Now I could understand with my mind and feel with my heart what he meant.

I was eager to do something that would awaken the same feelings of reverence and appreciation in Americans across the land. For most of the trip across the country I thought the beautiful places we visited were just tourist destinations. It wasn't until we were in Yellowstone and I saw the sign Yellowstone National Park and recalled that Acadia and Badlands both had those words behind them that I asked the fateful question, "What the heck is a national park?"

When I found out that there is an entire system of national parks that span the country from Alaska to the US Virgin Islands and beyond, I was astounded. Next I learned that it included not only the spectacular natural places like we'd seen, but also many of the places where significant events in American history happened.

A little more research revealed that the park system is maintained by the taxes all Americans pay. The mission statement says, "The National Park Service preserves unimpaired the natural and cultural resources and values of the National Park System for the enjoyment, education and inspiration of this and future generations."

Well obviously they were failing miserably at serving this generation, because for the entire journey across the country we'd seen only a handful of Black people in the parks. One was a young woman in Acadia who told us she was on a bus trip from New York. I met a Black woman in the bathroom in Olympic and Frank told me he saw a Black man there as well. I caught sight of one other Black person somewhere, before I realized it was a rare sighting. We saw no Hispanic people and no Native Americans, except for a few selling jewelry outside Grand Canyon.

Yet we'd seen hundreds of thousands of White Americans and many tour groups of European and Japanese people. How could this possibly be? The census said America's population was increasingly becoming more Black and brown. Since I didn't know about the parks and neither did any of my friends, how could the parks possibly be preserved for "this and future generations"?

Frank and I decided we needed to do something to make a change. We'd read the statement somewhere, "Instead of complaining about the dark, light a candle." So we decided that's just what we would do. Maybe I was unconsciously inspired by the Rev. Lester Davy's example.

We had some talent, since I was a journalist and Frank was an attorney and businessman. A year earlier we'd formed a company, Earthwise Productions, Inc., intending to publish an uplifting periodical, but we hadn't done anything with it. Now we saw clearly what we needed to do.

We'd produce a monthly newsletter sharing information about the parks and showing images of ourselves having a great time. That would have the benefit not only of providing information, but also of reassuring people that it was a safe and enjoyable experience.

Our first issue of Pickup & GO! rolled off the press November 1995, and we mailed the first 3,000 copies to friends and relatives and invited them to subscribe at $25 for 12 issues. We expected an enthusiastic response and – it didn't come. We got one subscription back.

Now we were at a crossroads. The desire to move to Belize had waned in the face of our big discovery. We had invested a chunk of our savings in the trip and now in the publication. Something needed to be done and we had the information and the capability to do it. But, if the people we thought would benefit most from it were uninterested, what was the point?

Frank pointed out that in marketing a 10 percent response is considered good, especially the first time out. I couldn't calculate what percentage 1 out of 3,000 was, but I felt a determination to keep going. How would things change if we didn't change them?

For months we kept writing and publishing and mailing. We subsidized our business with our income. One friend jokingly told me that if we weren't making money it was a hobby, not a business. Ouch! Well, it was a mission.

One night we went to a meeting of the local Broward County Audubon Society where we were the only Black members. A young woman from the Miami Audubon office was the guest speaker, and to our amazement she informed the group of a plan to restore the Everglades, a major breeding ground for birds. She said it would be the largest restoration project ever in history and would cost $5 billion.

She laid out how the Everglades was the source of South Florida's drinking water and said that, with the population rapidly increasing, we needed to recover and store the water that was being drained off to sea.

Frank had told me about the great hurricane of 1947 when he was 10 years old living in Dania, the very city where this meeting was being held. He said the flooding killed hundreds of people and animals in the agricultural areas farther west, and he'd actually seen fish swimming in the water down US 1, almost a mile away from the ocean.

He said that not long afterward, Congress ordered the US Army Corps of Engineers to make sure such a thing never happened again. He'd been there when the Corps oversaw the dredging of canals to drain the water out to sea, which also created dry land for development. Now here we were 50 years later, facing the consequences of that remedy, which had created its own problem.

The young Audubon woman said that the success of the restoration would depend upon how much the residents of South Florida supported it. She made a point of emphasizing the need for the Black and Hispanic community to get on board.

Frank and I looked at each other, eyes glowing. Surely our ship had come in. Here was a problem we were definitely qualified to help with. The centerpiece of the Everglades is Everglades National Park, and we knew the national parks as well as, or better than, most people.

Moreover, we knew how to communicate with the Black community and had direct access to them through the Westside Gazette. Frank had deep roots in South Florida so it would be relatively easy to get the information to community leaders and the general public in a way that would spark their interest.

But it was a much bigger challenge than we expected. We reached out to the Audubon Society and the government agencies in charge of the project, offering our consulting and communication services. But, while there was money for engineers and planners and other mostly-White professionals, there was no budget for communications that had been identified as so vitally important. Go figure.

We would not be deterred. The only organization that paid any attention to us was the National Audubon Society Ecosystem Restoration Office in Miami, where the director, Dr. Stuart Strahl, had recently returned from a post in South America. Maybe that experience made him more open to the inclusion of non-White people.

Once we went to a meeting of the Sierra Club and when we walked in the door, a perky White lady came up and greeted us.

"What brings you here?" she asked.

"My truck," Frank responded curtly.

She may not have intended to be insulting, but it sure sounded as if she thought we didn't belong. For the most part, people in the environmental field acted as if we were anomalies, and maybe they thought that if they didn't encourage us we would naturally become discouraged and go away.

Some people actually said to us, "Well, you know, Black people have so many survival issues, they don't have time to care about the environment. They have to think about paying the rent, the light bill...."

How they missed the daggers in my eyes I'll never know. My first retort was that yes, that may be true for some Black people, and it's also true for some White people. BUT I'M STANDING RIGHT HERE IN FRONT OF YOU AND I'M BLACK!! AND I PROBABLY KNOW MORE ABOUT THE REALITY OF NATURE FROM EXPERIENCING IT THAN YOU EVER WILL FROM READING ABOUT IT!!

Thank God for Frank. Calm, cool and collected, he'd pull me back from the edge. He had a lifetime of dealing with such prejudice and this was my first up-close experience.

I used to wonder what people meant when they talked about "the system." What kind of system could affect you everywhere? But now I saw the pervasive existence of low expectations and lack of investment in Black and Brown people and the effect it could have. Here we were offering our peerless, unique gifts and what we were getting felt like lumps of coal.

Still, we made a point of going to the meetings and writing about what we learned. The Westside Gazette published everything we wrote, and our friend Rodney Baltimore, a DJ at Hot 105.1 was so intrigued, he had us on his program frequently.

And that's when the other shoe dropped.

CHAPTER THIRTEEN

When we saw the plans for the urban side of the restoration project called Eastward Ho!, it set our hair on fire. The plan projected that, by the year 2020, the downtown corridor on the east side, from Orlando to Key West, would mostly be inhabited by young affluent White people who would live above the new upscale shops and cafes. The historically Black downtown areas where mostly Black people lived were in the bull's eye for development, gentrification that would price them out of the market.

Now I felt like every waking moment had to be devoted to letting people know what was coming. We wrote countless articles, got on radio, talked to politicians, homeowners, civic and business groups. We gave them the information we had just received. President Clinton had issued an Environmental Justice Order which required that any environmental project that would affect minorities must take into account their needs. We tried to show the Black community, the relevant government agencies, and the nonprofit environmental sector that this Order, if applied, could benefit everyone.

By 1997 we got small contracts with Audubon and the Water Management District which helped keep our work going. I was a little surprised, but definitely pleased, when Frank said to the leaders in one meeting,

"My wife doesn't understand the word 'no.' She thinks you must mean, 'not right now,' because she's not asking for anything extraordinary. She's just asking that you do what's fair."

I don't doubt that my stock went up among them to see the confidence my husband has in me.

Things took a dramatic turn later that year when we got a call from Ozone Action in Washington DC, asking us to help get the word out about a meeting they were planning to hold in Dania. They had been referred to us by Frank's buddy, Congressman Alcee Hastings, lifelong friends since they met at Howard University Law School in the 1950s.

The representatives from Ozone Action talked about the fact that Americans are only five percent of the world's population, yet consume 25 percent of all its resources and produce 40 percent of the waste! They said this was creating a huge problem in the climate which was leading to rapidly rising sea levels.

They warned that small countries which contribute least to the problem would suffer the most. To drive the point home, they'd flown in the Prime Minister of St. Kitts and Nevis who said they were already losing as much as a foot of beach every year, due to rising seas.

As an islander from the Caribbean living on a peninsula in the U.S., I found this very alarming. Now we redoubled our efforts to inform and warn people of what was coming. We encouraged the groups to whom we talked to organize and go to their City and County Commission meetings and raise their concerns. Frank emphasized that the Zoning and Planning Committees were particularly important because that's where many of the decisions were made that affect the environment and the future.

"All politics is local," he quoted Congressman Tip O'Neal.

Our philosophy was that we should do everything we could to get the results we want, but we shouldn't be attached to the results which were out of our control. Lucky for us, because the response we were getting was far below what we expected.

After a while we developed a reputation as committed environmentalists (or environmentalists who should be committed?). We had support in a few White environmental groups and developed some close friendships. To the majority though, it appeared we were a tiresome nuisance.

Once a White "leader" actually said to me derisively, "Well Audrey, we know you can't be discouraged."

Huh? I didn't know that people were trying to discourage me. And why?

We finally made a connection with the National Parks Conservation Association in Washington, DC, which advocated for the national parks. They had recently employed a Black woman to be their Cultural Diversity Director. Iantha Gantt-Wright and I bonded instantly and became lifelong friends.

She made contact with multiple Black, Hispanic, Asian and Native American leaders around the country who were active in the environmental sector. She raised money to bring us all together in DC where we made plans to hold the first conference on diversity in the national parks and forest systems.

"A Mosaic in Motion" was convened in San Francisco in 1997, attracting more than 600 people. We followed that up with conferences in Santa Fe, New Mexico and one in Atlanta, GA. Out of these conferences grew a solid network of Black and Brown environmental advocates from coast to coast. All of these people were passionate about the Earth and caring for God's creation.

For the Chieftess of the Gullah Geechee Nation, Queen Quet, climate change and sea level rise were already a clear and present danger. The Sea Islands off the U.S. mainland from North Carolina to Florida, on which her people had lived for almost 400 years, were being eaten away by the sea. Her people have their own language, which is very similar to the Jamaican dialect, and have retained their African traditions of living close to nature.

The changing climate was affecting everything from their land to their diet which was mostly centered on seafood. The Gullah Geechee people were adapting by using bags of oyster and clam shells to reinforce the shoreline.

That same year Frank and I decided to go to Jamaica to visit my Auntie B and my birthplace. I wanted Lisa and my two-year old grandson Yero to know where they come from. We had a wonderful reunion with my family, including Auntie B and several grandchildren she was raising, and visited Mama's grave with Cousin Blanche.

After being greeted over and over with love and thanks to God that I had come back, we proceeded to the ancestral home. No one was home and the four of us walked down to the gully behind the house. As we trudged through the luxurious overgrowth, I felt eyes on us. Looking up, I saw a strange man with a stern look on his face.

"Good morning. How are you?" I chirped.

"Very well, thank you."

"Are we trespassing?"

"I believe you are."

"Sorry! My name is Ruby and . . ."

"Ruby that went to Clarendon College and then went to work at Gleaner Company and then went away to America and never come back?"

Got me! My whole history in a nutshell. Clearly I was home.

Our work had begun to attract some notice, and in 1997 the National Parks Conservation Association gave us the Marjory

Stoneman Douglas Conservationist of the Year Award. Thankfully it came with a $5,000 check which helped sustain our work. At the turn of the century, Frank and I individually received the Environmental Hero Award from Vice President Al Gore and the National Oceanic and Atmospheric Administration.

That year I was invited to serve on several national Boards. I'm fairly certain that besides being the only Black person or person of color at those Board tables, I was among very few "thousandaires" among several multi-millionaires and a few billionaires.

In meetings I'd offer a well thought-out, logical and passionate plea to provide information to the public about the parks, with images that included Black and Brown people having a wonderful time. I'd emphasize how the census projected that by 2020 these ethnic groups would be a majority, and so it was imperative that they get to know the parks and fall in love with them as we had. I said we were presiding over the demise of the park system, if we failed to awaken the population that would be needed to support them in the future.

"Since Congress has to allocate the funds that support the parks and more people of color are being elected to Congress, why would they vote to put money into places that don't benefit their communities when they have urgent issues such as education, housing and jobs to fund?" I asked.

It became almost laughable to me that my fellow Board members would listen politely until I was finished, then there'd be a pause for a few moments, and the conversation would pick up right where we left off before I spoke.

Once a colleague said, "Well, just because we have a Pollyanna attitude and think everything is going to turn out fine, doesn't mean that it will."

I smiled sweetly and said, "Well, just because we sit here and talk and do nothing about the problem, doesn't mean it will either."

My refusal to be intimidated impressed some of my peers. One wealthy woman who became our friend and helped support our work asked me one day, "How do you have the courage to say the things you say?"

"Well, I have a whole lot of people behind me," I responded. "I'm speaking for millions who will never have the opportunity to make their voice heard. Besides, there are more people like me than people who're super wealthy, so I won't be intimidated."

The gentleman of the Pollyanna comment became one of our best friends and most ardent supporters.

Then I was invited to serve on the newly-formed Diversity Advisory Board of Delaware North Parks and Resorts, a concessionaire which manages lodging and amenities in many national parks. Our first meeting was held in Yosemite National Park.

This time, instead of sleeping by the side of the road, we had luxury quarters in the Ahwahnee Hotel, a historic and very elegant hotel where Queen Elizabeth, President John F. Kennedy, and later President Obama and the First Family stayed.

In 2003 we held our meeting at Cape Canaveral, which Delaware North also managed. To my amazement, I found myself seated at dinner between astronauts James Lovell and Wally Schirra. I did not know who they were until they were called up to speak.

These gentlemen had performed the first rendezvous of two capsules in outer space. They talked about the beauty of the Earth as they'd seen it from space, its exquisite fragility, and its small size floating in an ocean of nothingness.

One said that, at a certain point in space, he could put his thumb up to the window of his craft and it obscured the entire planet. They cautioned that, in order to protect our planetary home, we urgently needed to begin doing more to reduce the amount of pollution we were putting into the atmosphere.

I almost wept with the poignancy of the moment. Here I was seated between two humans who'd actually seen the Earth from outside itself. And Frank and I had seen so much of the Earth, its beauty and fragility, across so many differing landscapes. I was overcome with the feeling that humanity had been given a great treasure – literally the Garden of Eden – and we were wantonly and selfishly destroying it. It strengthened me to continue to do everything I could to wake up my fellow men and women to the awesome privilege and responsibility we have to enjoy and protect our home.

On our tour I actually got to touch the space shuttle which was under repair and we were driven out to the launch pad to see where the launches take off. One of the few regrets I have in life is that I failed to hold onto the great picture of me posed between these two incredibly accomplished men after it appeared in The Westside Gazette.

By this time Frank had accepted a job in Atlanta, the "Black Mecca," to head up the Southeastern office of The Wilderness Society. We hadn't even heard of this organization until we met one of its vice presidents at a conference in Asheville, North Carolina some years before. The Society protects wilderness areas in the national parks and forests, where motorized vehicles are barred and you can only enter under your own steam. The idea is to make sure some wild places are left untouched for future generations.

Frank's job was to work with the local community and engage them to help conserve wilderness areas. His duties included building relationships with Black Members of Congress so he was frequently in DC. Our representative was Congressman John Lewis who had been beaten almost to the point of death in the Civil Rights movement and jailed multiple times.

Frank had been a leader in the movement in Florida so he had that in common with many of the venerable Black members of Congress, including Representatives James Clyburn, Elijah Cummings and his old friend Alcee Hastings. They all marveled that it was the first time they were seeing a Black man representing an environmental organization on Capitol Hill.

Things were a little different in the Atlanta environmental community where groups were starkly divided between Black and White. There were Black leaders including Dr. Na'Taki Osborne-Jelks and Felicia Davis of the West Atlanta Watershed Alliance who were way out front, having conserved hundreds of acres of forest in their neighborhood, just 10 minutes from downtown Atlanta.

But when we went to environmental justice meetings where people were dealing with the effects of pollution and the suffering it caused their families from asthmatic children and lost wages and high hospital bills, almost all the people in attendance were Black. When we went to meetings where Frank was representing the Wilderness Society that included, for example, members of Ted Turner's family, nearly all the people attending were White.

The funniest experience we had was in North Georgia, where residents had reached out to the Wilderness Society for help to protect forest lands in the area. The meeting was being held at a restaurant and bar. When we drove up we felt that little tingle of unease you get when you're out of your element.

The area was predominantly White and rural, the restaurant was rustic, and we did not see a Black face anywhere. We walked in and Frank introduced himself to a gentleman as the Director of the Wilderness Society. The look on that gentleman's face was priceless. He actually looked behind us – I guess for the REAL wilderness guy – but he soon recovered, and Frank told me they had an amicable and productive meeting. I sat in a booth and read while I waited.

****

CHAPTER FOURTEEN

In his first year, Frank helped spearhead a grassroots group called "Keeping It Wild" which sought to bridge the chasm between Black and White environmental organizations. The group organized outings to national parks and forests in the Atlanta area, as Frank reasoned that the best way to develop a constituency to support nature was to expose people to the natural resources in their own backyard.

Many of the leaders were Black, which was a big draw to others in the urban area who happily joined in to go exploring, hiking, whitewater rafting and scuba diving. I reconnected with my friend Jennifer Ffrench from the Gleaner, who'd married wonderful Curtis Parker and founded The Crossroads News newspaper in Atlanta. Along with their daughters Jami and Kelli, they joined us for a weekend camping at Red Top Mountain State Park sponsored by Recreation Equipment Incorporated, REI, and supported all our efforts from then on.

Each year Keeping It Wild held a big Gala that brought all segments of the community together. Our first Keynote Speaker was Congressman John Lewis.

One great benefit of being in Atlanta was that Lisa lived there with our grandson Yero who was almost eight years old. For the first time in many years, my daughter and I were back living close together. If Yero wasn't feeling well or if Lisa - a teacher who specialized in instructing gifted students - had to go to work and Yero didn't have to go to school, I'd pick him up and we'd spend the day together.

I worked from home in our apartment on Piedmont Avenue facing the Civic Center, and we could walk to Piedmont Park or Centennial Olympic Park at our leisure. One day I picked up Yero and as he got into the backseat I heard him scream.

Frightened, I turned around and asked, "What's wrong?"

His little face was ashen as he pointed to a Sierra Club Magazine on the floor. The headline read, "30,000 trees cut down." He was so distressed.

"How will we get oxygen?" he asked.

Funny, Frank told me he had asked that same question in the 1940s, the day he saw the huge banyan tree outside his elementary school classroom being cut down.

"How will we get oxygen?"

It was becoming an urgent question, though only a few were aware.

In 2004 our new friend Bess Covington introduced me to Mahikari-no-Waza, the Japanese teaching of the Art of Divine Light. Groups of Kamikumites, students from all over North America and the world, were getting ready to journey to Japan to participate in The 45th Grand Anniversary Festival. Frank and I decided this was our perfect opportunity to visit Japan and joined Bess and our friend Barbara Jamison for the trip. We flew out of Atlanta and arrived in Narita 15 hours later.

To our amazement, when Frank and I stepped out of our hotel in Tokyo to go and explore the city, the first thing we heard was Bob Marley's "One Love" blaring from a huge projector in the square! What are the odds! We took the train underground and got off directly in an underground mall. Passing a shoe store I got excited at the sight of several attractive pairs of shoes and walked in excitedly. The young woman who greeted us looked at my feet and asked, "What size?"

"Nine," I responded eagerly.

"Soo sorry," she said gently. "We only go up to size seven."

Talk about feeling like a bull in a china shop. Frank still laughs about the look on my face.

Groups of Kamikumites toured the country on buses and Frank observed how efficiently the Japanese use all available lands – with fruits and vegetables growing in their front yard all the way into the towns. When we arrived at Su-Za where the festival would take place, we saw the main temple gleaming in the distance like a diamond in the sky. The services were scheduled to begin at 2 a.m. so we got up an hour earlier and joined thousands of people pouring into the temple. It was such an ecstatic spiritual experience that Bess, Barbara and I began singing, "Oh when the saints go marching in," and people around us happily joined in.

Next day we went to visit Mount Fuji National Park, and adored its gleaming snow covered peak from afar. Wow!

In 2005 when a tsunami washed away more than a quarter million people in Asia, I took it as a sign of things to come. I decided to find out where the issue was in the thinking of world leaders. I wasn't surprised to find that Nobel Peace Prize winners Wangari Maathai and the Dalai Lama were sounding the alarm, saying that the environment and our response to climate change was a neglected issue, and should have the highest priority.

What shocked and alarmed me was what I read from the scientists and the Pentagon.

The lead scientist on the Intergovernmental Panel on Climate Change, Dr. Rajendra Pachauri, had come out with a warning as if his hair was on fire. As a member of a profession known for being calm and deliberate, he was practically shrieking. His chief concern was the recent discovery that, because of inertia built into the Earth's system, we were only now seeing the effects of the pollution that we put into the atmosphere in the 1960s and 70s. He said that, with the pollution we discharged in the intervening decades which coincide with an industrial boom, the effects would be so horrific that we needed to immediately and drastically reduce the amount of pollution we created. He warned that we had maybe 10 years to make a meaningful change, if we were lucky.

To my amazement, while the public was almost ignorant of this looming existential threat, the Pentagon was busy making plans how to control the fallout. They foresaw water shortages in some parts of the world causing famine, war, mass displacement of people, and increased migration, and were creating strategic plans about how to deal with what they saw as inevitable.

A little knowledge can be dangerous, and here I had a lot of knowledge about something extremely dangerous, and only a limited means of getting the information out. I wondered why the Pentagon was not sounding the alarm to the people, given that they had both the information and the means to get it out.

Many environmental scholars such as Bill McKibben, who formed the organization 350.0rg, wrote books and articles and gave speeches warning of looming climate disaster. Magazines such as National Geographic and Sierra included articles about it, but the environmental community did not mobilize in a way significant enough to make people know that they personally were in jeopardy, as were future generations.

The lack of concern about how their actions would affect their descendants really surprised me. One family member told us outright that he didn't care because he'd be dead and gone.

"But your grandchildren," I sputtered.

It didn't make a difference. I couldn't understand how people professed to love their children and could look into their innocent eyes knowing the hellish future we were creating for them, and placidly do nothing about it. I found myself writing and saying bluntly that future generations will revile us and curse our name. I never dreamt that it would happen in my lifetime. Now it's in the news every day, with young people such as Greta Thunberg rightfully charging that we have stolen their dreams.

Thank God for the national parks, because they literally saved my sanity. One of the most memorable adventures we had took place in a remote area outside Dallas, Texas. When we recounted it to our friends later, one young man said,

"And you didn't kill each other? My wife and I would not have made it."

We laughed, but it had gotten truly scary.

I was going to a Board meeting in Dallas, Texas and Frank was coming with me. For years we'd wanted to visit the Big Thicket National Preserve and, although it was more than 200 miles away from where we were staying, we were excited to make the trip. Then an emergency came up involving Frank's mother Veta Mae and I had to fly to Ft. Lauderdale to help her. Frank went on ahead as we'd already paid for our flights.

I got to Dallas after midnight and woke up bright-eyed and bushy-tailed, ready for our adventure. We took off at 11 a.m. for the long, circuitous drive, much of it on two-lane highways. At 4 p.m. we arrived at the Visitor Center, checked out the fascinating models of the ecosystem and its inhabitants, had a spirited conversation with a park ranger who knew of our work, and headed out to the Sundew Trail, which she said was her favorite.

"You'll see pitcher plants and lots of warblers and pileated woodpeckers," she said.

We'd passed the sign for that trail about seven miles up the road, but before we got back there we came to a sign for the Turkey Creek Trail. On a printout Frank gave me at the hotel that morning,

I'd read that this was a 1.5 mile loop trail. We turned off the highway and headed for Turkey Creek.

The parking lot was strangely deserted. While Frank got his binoculars and bug spray, I walked the few yards back to the highway and took a picture of the sign. I had no idea how fortuitous that would be in our later rescue.

The forest was so thick and the treetops so high, we could hear a lot of birds calling in the canopy but we couldn't see them. Suddenly, I saw a bright red, almost crimson bird land on a branch way up in a pine tree. As I trained my binoculars on it, a larger, greenish yellow bird perched nearby. Wow!

"The red one is a Scarlet Tanager," Frank said. "Oh, I think it's a pair. The other one is the female."

We were in instant rapture standing there in the quiet of the woods, with only the sounds of birds and scurrying animals all around. Mentally I was back on the banks of my gully.

As we continued walking I started thinking it was the longest 1.5 miles I'd ever seen. I didn't say anything to Frank because - what was the point? We were in the forest, we weren't meeting anyone else we could ask where the trail led, and sooner or later it would have to take us back to the parking lot, since it was a 'loop.'

But after what felt like five miles, I couldn't hold it in anymore.

"This trail is not 1.5 miles," I said.

"'Same thing I was thinking," he responded. 'But you saw in the printout that it was 1.5 miles, right?'

"Yes," I said confidently.

By now it felt like we were up to at least seven miles. The river that we'd seen on the left about 20 minutes into the forest was now on the right, then on the left, as the trail meandered up, down, and around. At points we could hear traffic, which meant we were relatively close to a road, but then the trail would take us away from it.

Where had we gone wrong, we wondered. We hadn't seen any turnoffs, so we couldn't have gotten on a different trail. The trail was well maintained and open. Lucky, because that's when we saw the first snake.

It was a coral snake with those stripes I knew indicated it was poisonous. It was directly on the trail and Frank almost stepped on it before we saw it. Both he and the snake leapt into the air in surprise.

Whew! OK! So the sun was going down, there was no end to the trail in sight, we had no water, food, light or first aid, and now we had to watch out for snakes. Frank had his iPhone but no signal.

We kept plodding on, keeping our conversation light and optimistic. What does this experience teach us, we asked? Duh! Obviously, never to go on a new trail without a map, and never to go hiking without a compass and basic necessities such as water, a few snack bars, a first aid kit, and always to get information about the trail before we get on it.

Suddenly Iantha's voice came to mind. "Call to Archangel Chamuel, sis," she always tells me whenever I'm looking for something. Invariably I've found that when I remember to call to unseen realms for assistance, help immediately shows up.

So I made the call verbally, out loud, "Beloved God, beloved Archangel Chamuel, finder of lost things, please help us find the highway. I accept it done, and thank you."

Frank regularly meditates and prays so I knew that he too was internally calling for assistance.

Then his phone rang! Whoa! We must be close to civilization! At least we'd be able to get a message to the park to find out how long this trail really was, and where it was taking us.

"Hello? Hello?' Frank said.

But there was nobody on the line.

Suddenly the forest erupted with the tune from the Twilight Zone! Somebody else is in here with us, we thought. But it was Frank's phone going nuts. I asked him if that had ever happened before and he said, "Never."

With dark descending, I was pleasantly surprised to find that I was feeling no fear or apprehension. I focused on what it would feel like when we got into our room at the luxurious Dallas Hyatt.

And at that moment, Frank saw a post marker with a sign, "1 mile." Thank you, God! We were only one mile away from somewhere – which meant a parking lot, a trail head, something. With a renewed burst of energy we took off at a good clip. We usually walk a mile in 12 minutes and it was now 10 minutes to 8, with sundown likely around 8 p.m.

I do not have the words to describe our amazement, delight and gratitude when we emerged from the woods into a parking lot a few minutes later. Thank you, God! Now, where is our car?!

Right away it was evident that this was not the same trailhead where we had entered. Walking out to the street, we saw a sign a little farther ahead and began walking towards it, in the hope that that was where we had left the car. Several vehicles flew by us, and I wondered what their occupants made of two Black people walking way out in the boonies at dusk.

A young White man came barreling down a side street and made eye contact with us as he waited at the Stop sign. I waved to him and he pulled over and asked, "Do you all need help?"

"Yes!" I screamed.

When we told him what had happened and that we were looking for our car, he said he didn't know where we were talking about, but invited us to hop in and he'd try to help us find it. Frank told him right away that we would happily pay him.

By now it was dark, and we hurtled down the country road to the first place he thought we might have parked. But no, that wasn't it. Then I remembered the picture I'd taken of the trail sign, and when I showed it to him, he said, "Oh, I think I know where that is."

So we went flying through the dark again, turning onto a dirt road and driving about 15 minutes.

I asked him what he thought when he saw us and he said, "Oh, I just thought you all needed help, and I wanted to help you. I'd want someone to help me if I need it. There are a lot of people around here who are very rude."

Well, thank God we met a Good Samaritan who was both polite and helpful. About 20 minutes after he picked us up, he wheeled onto the main road and there was our trail head and our car! Thank you, God!

Frank gave him $40 over his protests that we didn't have to give him that much, while we were like, "Oh yes, we do!"

Driving back to Dallas in the dead of night, we couldn't stop thinking how miraculous the whole experience had been. How did we get out of the forest just before dark, when our chances would have plummeted to zero? Two minutes later and we'd have missed our Good Samaritan. And how fortuitous was it that I'd taken a picture of that sign?

But the best and most amazing blessing of all was to find that, when the chips were down, neither Frank nor I gave into fear, blame, or bickering. We worked together and kept our focus, tuned into our spiritual nature and called for spiritual help.

When we checked the printout later, it said Turkey Creek Trail was a 15-mile linear trail! It was actually the Pitcher Plant Trail that was 1.5 miles! Chalk it up to my arrogance or fatigue. We pledged that, wherever we were going, we'd make sure we'd be better prepared from then on.

Another incredible adventure took place on Cumberland Island National Seashore in Georgia. In the 1800s, the Rockefellers and Carnegies and Vanderbilts had their summer estates on this island, and the Black people who served them lived on the North End 15 miles away. They walked to work every day and walked back at night.

The island is famous for the hundreds of wild horses that live there. We really wanted to see them, and knew enough to be careful, to try not to startle them, or get past their comfort zone. Surprisingly, they allowed us to get to within 20 to 30 feet.

Frank was taking pictures of the horses on the marsh and I climbed up on a sand dune and ducked into a grove of small trees. Less than 10 feet in I found myself at the edge of a clearing where three big horses were sharing an intimate moment. One was rolling around on his back in the golden sand. Another was nuzzling a mare that was facing my direction.

In a split second the horses went from playful abandon to rigid surprise. The one on the ground rolled and sprang up and all three trained their full attention on me. I saw the stallions' ears go back and knew that meant danger.

One moment I was calling Frank to come and get this real nature picture and the next I was walking on my heels, backing into the bushes I'd come through. I didn't stop moving until I put a reasonable distance between us.

Later that afternoon we saw the same two stallions and the mare grazing by the edge of the marsh. Suddenly, the bigger stallion dropped the other horse to his knees with a tremendous kick.

While our attention was riveted on that scene, I heard a noise and, just like in a movie, a chestnut horse came galloping full speed across the dunes, its mane flying. Frank was standing ahead of me, focusing on getting a shot of the other horses. As he snapped a picture of the smaller stallion swiftly nipping the dominant male, he saw the horse racing directly at him.

For a heart-stopping moment, I wondered what he would do. If he moved in any direction the horse might try to correct its course and they could easily collide. Frank stood there calmly and the horse flashed past him, no more than a foot away.

I know that at that moment both our faces were transfigured. The Earth, in its innumerable indescribable forms and all upon it, was a source of unending wonder and joy.

A few years later, we organized a tour of historic sites focused on the contributions of Black Americans for a group of people from Fort Lauderdale including NBC TV anchor Julia Yarbough and producer Monica Robinson. On Cumberland Island, the Superintendent organized a trip up to the North End community where the African Americans used to live. He let us into the small First African Baptist Church that our ancestors had built and where they'd worshipped over many years, and where John F. Kennedy, Jr. married Caroline Bissett Kennedy. We gathered behind the pulpit and sang "We HAVE overcome," with great gusto and thanksgiving to our forebears who had endured so much and got us the opportunities we now enjoy.

Another time when we went back to Yellowstone, I crept out of bed one morning while Frank was still asleep and headed out to Old Faithful. I wanted to see the geyser as near dawn as I could. As I was going out the door the young woman behind the desk called out to me, "Watch out for moose!" I wondered why moose, since there were bison and bears around too.

I walked out into the cold crisp air and made my way to the geyser just a stone's throw away, keeping my head on a swivel. When I got there I found myself alone, and exulted in praise to the great glorious God who enabled me to have such amazing experiences. I could see my beloved and most favorite constellation Orion blazing in the sky, just like I'm accustomed to seeing it in

Fort Lauderdale or wherever I am. How big is that thing, I joked to myself.

I could see the constellation Cassiopeia as well. I called out to her and made a special wish. Then I added, "And if it is your will, please show me a sign that it will be granted."

Suddenly I heard the sound of music coming across the fields. It was clear and pure, as if someone was out there playing a flute. Then I realized it was the elk bugling, the males making the sound they use to attract females in mating season. Wow!

As it got lighter, a group of people came up, talking animatedly with each other. One gentleman went to set up his tripod in an area where I'd seen the boiling water reach the day before, so I told him that was not safe. Hearing my accent he asked,

"Are you from Jamaica?"

When I said yes he went on, "Do you know a guy name Wilmot Perkins? I ...."

I didn't hear the rest of what he said over the sound of the blood pounding in my head. I'd met Wilmot "Mutty" Perkins while I worked at the Gleaner. Wow! What are the odds of an Englishman and a Jamaican woman meeting up in Yellowstone and calling the name of someone we both know in Jamaica? We're a small country, but not that small.

I took it as a sign that my request had been heard and would be granted, and I carry that nugget in my heart at all times like a security blanket. Thank You, God!

About an hour's drive away from Yellowstone is the Grand Teton National Park, my top favorite of all the national parks we've visited. Driving along the John D. Rockefeller Memorial Parkway which connects them, you suddenly come upon a wall of snowcapped mountains, so high that they seem to touch the sky. There are seven peaks and the middle one, known as the Royal Teton, has sported a patch of cloud around it, like an ellipse, all five times I've visited. They're often called the "Oh! My! God!" mountains because that's all you can think or say when you see them.

There's a river running at their feet, and between the river and the parkway are meadows which in the summer are an indescribable panorama of blooms, lupines in yellow, red and purple. Once we took a group of friends on a tour of Yellowstone and Grand Teton and when she saw that view, one woman fell back in her seat and exclaimed,

"All this beauty is wearing me out!"

Grand Teton is in Wyoming, one of the Whitest states in the Union. So when I was coming out of my cabin upon arrival one day and ran into a group of Black women who turned out to be Jamaican, you can imagine the reunion that ensued. There was only one man in the group, and they told me they are recruited by a company that brings them to the U.S. every year to work as housekeepers in the national parks. It makes me so happy to know that some of my Jamaican countrymen and women are getting to experience these fabulous places.

Mama, Mrs. Ida Butler

My birth home is still standing

Mom, Avenel Joyce Butler

Papa, Mr. Joseph Wright

Iron with coal inside

Coal stove with irons

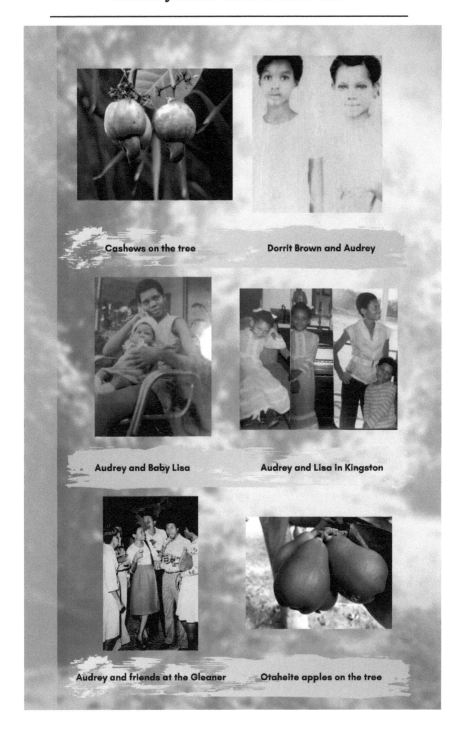

Cashews on the tree

Dorrit Brown and Audrey

Audrey and Baby Lisa

Audrey and Lisa in Kingston

Audrey and friends at the Gleaner

Otaheite apples on the tree

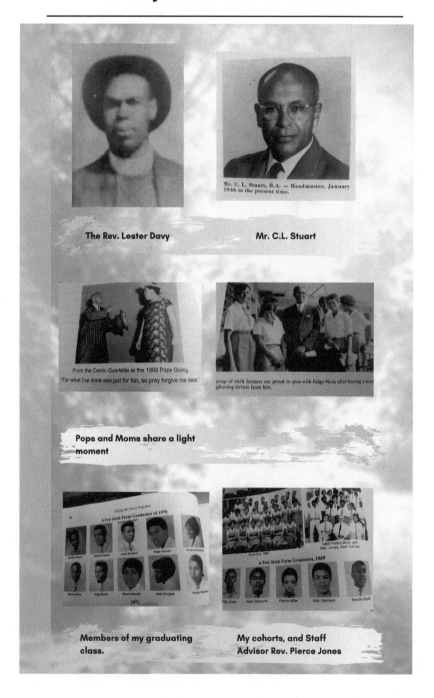

The Rev. Lester Davy

Mr. C.L. Stuart

From the Comic Quartette at the 1969 Prize Giving
"For what I've done was just for fun, so pray forgive me dear."

group of sixth formers are proud to pose with Judge Myrie after hearing a most ightening lecture from him.

Pops and Moms share a light moment

Members of my graduating class.

My cohorts, and Staff Advisor Rev. Pierce Jones

Cousin Braddie and family in Holland

Veta Mae at my 50th birthday party

Audrey at Grand Canyon National Park

Audrey and Frank in Denali, Alaska

Audrey and Frank, Yosemite, California

Audrey, Lisa and Grandson Yero

Meeting Robert Redford

With Susan Taylor, Essence Magazine

With Dr, Erieka Bennett and Lou Gossett Jr.

Interviewing Patti LaBelle

With Astronaut Story Musgrave

Dr. Musgrave outside Earth

With Nobel Prize Winner
Wangari Maathai

With Dr. Sylvia Earle

Interviewing National
Park Service Director
Robert Stanton

Frank, Al Calloway, South Florida Times
publishers Robert and Michelle Beatty,
Prof. Ta-Shana Taylor, Nicole in Everglades

Westside Gazette publisher Bobby
Henry and grandsons Bryce and Bobby
III visit the Everglades

Meeting Ranger Betty Reid
Soskin

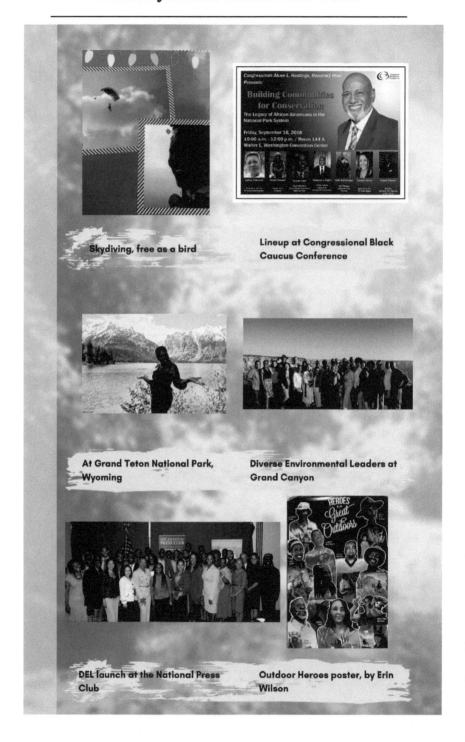

Skydiving, free as a bird

Lineup at Congressional Black Caucus Conference

At Grand Teton National Park, Wyoming

Diverse Environmental Leaders at Grand Canyon

DEL launch at the National Press Club

Outdoor Heroes poster, by Erin Wilson

With American Hiking Society repairing trail in Golden Gate, California

Informing Natural Resource subcommittee in Congress

Auntie B in pink, with her children Marsha, Karen and Victor Manning

My cousin Judith Johnson, Auntie B's daughter, in Maine

Grandson Yero on cover of Outdoor Retailer Magazine, Spring 2019

Asheville event with Pathways to Parks and allies

Frank and Audrey in the Blue and John Crow Mountains National Park

Beating Blue Mountain coffee in a mortar

Roasting cashews with the twins

My gully lives!

Cousin Lillian Canacee finds a rock for her garden

Ms. Thomas again after 60 years!

Me and Frank enjoying Limitless

Uncle Ricky visiting us on Limitless

My breadfruit tree is still bearing

Cocoa pod on our property

Guineps from Sheena's tree

Farmer Simpson's gifts of plantains, breadfruit and avocados

CHAPTER FIFTEEN

Having Frank in my life is like having a permanent ace in the hole. Once we were visiting Alaska and a minor emergency came up which required an immediate change of plans. I instinctually made a quick decision that worked out perfectly. My very wealthy friend who was also involved asked me later,

"Were you always so confident, or did you become more confident since you married Frank?"

I thought about it and really couldn't decide. I told her I remember always being self-assured, though I'm probably more confident being with Frank, because I know he always has my back and he has never given me a moment's worry. This is not to say that he won't gently point out to me when he thinks I'm wrong, emphasis on gently.

Early in our marriage, I still had the Jamaican characteristic of being late for everything. If I was only 15 minutes late I considered that being on time. I told Frank that was part of our culture and cited the pantomime "8 O'clock Jamaica Time" which used to begin at 8:30 p.m. Pantomimes resonate with me especially because my former boss on The Star, Mrs. Gloudon, wrote many of them.

But Frank had an entirely different relationship with time and liked to arrive a few minutes early. This was completely inconceivable to me. One day when we were going out and Frank was once again dressed and waiting patiently for me, I said to him, "Well, why can't YOU be late sometimes?"

The moment the words left my mouth I regretted them, because it sounded so asinine even to my ears.

But he only smiled. "Honey, time is fixed, it's a covenant we make with others in society that allows us to coordinate ...."

"I know that," I snapped haughtily.

"Well, when you are late you are showing the other person that you have no respect for their time, because they have to waste their time waiting for you."

Yikes! That hit home. From that day I made every effort never to be late and, if I have to be late or am somewhat delayed, I call as soon as I know so the other person is not held up waiting for me. Plus, he said nothing bad ever happened to him from being early, but a lot could happen from being late, including the stress of rushing to compensate for an unexpected traffic or other delay.

When we got married, I was already in my 40s and somewhat set in my ways. I'd go out on an assignment for the Gazette or out with my friends and all Frank asked was that, if I was going to be out longer than expected, I should call and let him know. I bristled at that of course, "I'm not a child. I don't have to report to anyone."

Calmly, patiently, he said, "Well, think about how you'd feel if I was out and you didn't know where I was or when I'd be coming home."

Okay, I could see that perspective. I immediately made the change and it didn't feel onerous at all.

One of the first Black lawyers in St Petersburg, Florida in the 1960s, Frank and his first wife Peggy Peterman went to Howard University together. She became a highly respected journalist, one of the first Black women columnists at the St. Petersburg Times newspaper.

When we first met, they had been divorced for many years and Frank was on a one-year hiatus from his second wife. They'd given each other that time to determine if they could work out their differences.

Frank told me that, when he was driving Peggy and their two young sons Frank Jr. and John from Florida to Tuskegee, Alabama to visit her parents in the 1960s, he kept a pistol on his dashboard. He said it was a signal to White racists who might want to harass them.

"I was going to protect my family," he said. "So my message was, 'You can come over here but you're going to get something you might not like.' "

I was stunned because at that time, as a carefree girl in Jamaica, I had no concept of that kind of vicious racism. The fact that someone so close to me had gone through it was really shocking.

Frank was widely respected in St. Petersburg where he'd successfully represented several Black groups, one of which was Black police officers. When the St. Petersburg Police Department hired the first Black policemen, they severely restricted their activities. For example, they could arrest Black people, but not Whites. If they stopped a White person for any infraction, they had to call a White counterpart to come and talk to them or make an arrest. Not only was this demeaning and infuriating to the Black officers, but it also made them a laughing stock in the Black Community.

When a few police officers approached Frank and his law partners Jim Sanderlin and Frank White and told them they wanted to sue the City, he advised them what they needed to do. The group swelled to what became known as The Courageous Twelve and raised money for the lawsuit that Frank and the firm successfully brought against the City.

The second big victory came on behalf of the sanitation workers who were bargaining for better working conditions. He negotiated successfully on their behalf. When the City allowed a huge mural to be placed on the walls of City Hall, bearing caricatures of Black people with oversize lips and popping eyes, eating watermelon and dancing a jig, the Black community was outraged. Members of JOMO, the Junta of Military Organizations, took it upon themselves to go to City Hall and rip it down. The City promptly prosecuted them for felonies, and Frank and his law partners successfully defended them and got the charges reduced to misdemeanors. This guy!

Frank was also the first Black person to run for office in Pinellas County. Some of my favorite photos are of him sitting at a long table at a formal dinner where everyone else is an older White man. Frank looked like the only chocolate chip in the cookie. But I know he wasn't fazed. He was building up steam in the community, when his White opponent ran an ad in the papers bearing both their pictures with the caption, "Know your candidate." We still have that newspaper page.

Frank lost the election but years later his son, Frank Jr., was elected to the City Council and then represented the area in the

Florida State Legislature for two terms. Later he became the Secretary of Juvenile Justice under Governor Charlie Crist.

One of the things I love best about my husband is the way he takes care of himself, including his mental hygiene. He is an inveterate joker, and admits he can't help himself. His favorite book is *Psycho-Cybernetics* which he studies regularly, and *The Seven Spiritual Laws of Success* by Deepak Chopra. Because of Frank, I am often chagrined by the commercials and the general narrative that promotes the idea that men pass their peak at age 40 after which they need artificial help to perform sexually.

Once I was in my regular barbershop in Atlanta getting a haircut when one of those commercials came on. There were only a few people in the shop so I felt comfortable enough to say, "I don't understand why they want to put out the idea that a man passes his prime so young and needs help."

I expected my barber to say, "Yaay, I don't know why they do that."

But what he said instead was, "It's because we're working so hard...." and his friend at the next chair joined in with something similar.

Oh! Shut my mouth!

Still, I can't help myself. I try to tell our sons in a subtle way that they have a lot to look forward to and shouldn't buy into that negativity. I don't know if they get it, but at least I've done my part in trying to tell them that if they take care of themselves, they can have an active and satisfying life at least into their 80s where Frank is. When we read a report in an AARP magazine that older folks and retirees are having an improved love life with relations up to twice a month, we laughed out loud. In our world that would be a slow week.

For Frank's 80th birthday I threw him a big party in the revolving room of the Hyatt Pier 66 on Fort Lauderdale Beach that brought: his brother Jimmy and our sister-in-law Janice and their children; five of our six children; grand and great-grandchildren; lifelong friends Dr. Leaphart and Charles; the two Carolyns; Cammal; and Bob among many others, to celebrate him in grand style.

People often ask us, "How long have you guys been married?"

When we tell them close to 30 years, they're surprised.

"You still act like newlyweds. You say 'please' and 'thank you' to each other and treat each other so gently...."

Well, yes of course. Why would we choose to treat each other, the person that we're closest to, living together, sharing our lives, with any less respect than we'd treat a stranger? We are each other's dearest treasure.

It really helps that we have so much in common, beginning with the love and respect for nature. Frank is an avid writer, painter and sculptor. All the paintings we have in our little flat are his creation, rich in the primary colors of red, yellow and blue that we both love.

The other thing is that we both love words and strive to communicate exactly what we mean. Frank loves to joke, and sometimes if it doesn't hang together logically I ask him to break it down for me so I can understand. At that point he'll laugh and say, "Nothing worse than a joke that has to be explained" or "You don't get it unless I hit you over the head with a two by four."

I guess I am a little off center. I clearly remember my friend Norman Hall at the University of the West Indies teasing me that if someone yelled "Fire!" while everybody else was running I'd be looking around asking, "Where?"

I strive not to panic or engage a fear-based reaction just because others are caught up in it. I am often amazed at how quick people are to go negative. I was in a supermarket recently when a young White woman misplaced her cart. She immediately went into panic mode exclaiming that someone had "stolen" her cart. For a few moments she was so alarmed, acting as if she was under attack. A few minutes later when she found the cart two aisles over, it was as if she had overcome a huge threat. As far as I could see, there were only groceries in the cart that she had not yet paid for. I wanted to say to her "Lady, you know that you manufactured that entire 'crisis'? Imagine the amount of harmful hormones that were let loose in your body over nothing."

Still, I try to work at not being judgmental and giving others the benefit of the doubt. Once I was called up for jury duty in Atlanta. I was very excited at the opportunity to do my civic duty. When the potential jurors were being questioned, the attorney asked us whether, if we saw someone driving erratically on the highway, we'd think they were drunk. Everyone ahead of me said yes. When he got to me I said no, thinking how happy they'd be to have a juror who could be objective.

The lawyer seemed surprised and repeated the question. Again I said no, explaining that the person could have a medical emergency so I wouldn't just presume they were drunk. When he asked my profession and I responded that I'm an environmental consultant, the whole room looked at me as if I'd grown two heads. They threw me off the pool so fast. Oh well.

One Saturday morning soon after we moved to Atlanta it was drizzling and I felt like staying in bed, so Frank went for a walk by himself. When he came back about an hour later, he was very excited.

"Honey, I found this great place! You have to see it!"

Sure. Next day we walked to his new discovery, which turned out to be a quaint neighborhood called Virginia Highlands. As we were walking down the street looking in the shop windows, I saw a pair of gorgeous white culottes that were just coming back into fashion.

"Oh! I love those pants!" I squealed. "I'll have to come back and get them!"

"I thought you would," Frank said with satisfaction.

We went a few blocks farther and turned around, walking on the opposite side of the street.

Then I saw a pair of green outdoor pants with multiple pockets, in the same window.

"Oh!" I said, "I love those green pants! I have to come back and get them!"

"What are you talking about?" he asked, puzzled. "Didn't you just see those pants on your way down and say you love them?"

"No," I said. "I didn't see the green pants. I was talking about the white pants."

And just like that, we realized how incredibly complex communication is. I hadn't specified "white" earlier, so he assumed I was talking about the green pants which he'd noticed and I hadn't even seen. Looking in the same store window and thinking we were talking about the same thing, we were actually talking about two completely different things. If we were an adversarial couple, we might have gotten into an argument from such a simple misunderstanding.

It illustrated to us that meaning doesn't come out of one person's head and go directly into the other person's. It's affected by a lot of things that the communications expert Marshall McLuhan called "noise in the channel," composed of our experiences and perceptions that cause us to interpret things one way or the other.

From then on, whenever we find ourselves talking at cross-purposes or not understanding each other, we say, "White pants, green pants." That is our signal to stop and start over.

I shared that example at a conference where I was speaking shortly after, and the audience roared. Afterwards an older White gentleman came up to me and said, "Thank you. You just gave me the key to understanding my wife."

I'm not sure what he meant, but it was evidently a good thing.

Another best thing about Frank is that he doesn't expect others to be like him. Where someone else might get frustrated and say, "Why didn't you do it the way I'd do it?" Frank's approach is always, "You didn't do it the way I would do it because you're not me. And who says my way is better than yours?"

What a great guy! Men love him as much as women do, because he's so mellow. I love the influence he has on younger men, as he's always perfectly well turned out and elegant. Visiting the campus of Morehouse College where he went to school in the 1950s I was so proud to see his picture on the wall with the Class of '58, "The

Mighty Seventeen," including nuclear physicist Walter Massey who was President of the College 1995-2007. Young men are always eager to be around him and hear his stories.

Once I overheard our eleven-year-old grandson Cameron Suber who's so gifted that he builds computers and robs from scratch and plays the French Horn asking, "Grandpa, how did you get to be so cool?"

Frank laughed and said, "I just take it one day at a time, son. One day at a time. And I know everything changes and will pass so I don't worry."

Many times at a hotel bar or in conversation with a stranger, young men will ask us what's our secret to being happily married. I always tell them the "three of us in the relationship" and "both of you shouldn't go crazy at the same time" stories.

Frank said I also brought gifts that help him with his attitude. Walking down the streets of Atlanta, for example, he noticed I said hello to everyone whose eyes I met. Sometimes people spoke in response and sometimes they didn't. I told him I didn't care whether they responded or not, I was only interested in doing my part - acting as one human being to another.

I told him how, growing up in Jamaica, if you pass the same person three times in one day you say hello each time. He told me that growing up in Dania he'd been the same way, but when he went to the city and realized how many people didn't speak in return, he stopped doing it.

Now he said, "Thank you for reminding me that I am not responsible for how other people act, just how I behave."

The other great lesson he taught me was not to take on every problem. I have an opinion about everything and feel passionately that I have to be involved to help create positive change. But Frank reminded me, "Honey, stay in your lane. Do what you can in your area of expertise, but you can't solve every problem. It will drive you crazy to try."

Well, duh! Of course. He really helped me focus and stop dissipating my energy in all directions.

I came to see my energy as a ball, 360 degrees round. I tell people in my audience, especially young people, that I guard my energy jealously in order to be most effective.

"If I give five percent of my energy to anger, another five percent to grief, jealousy, or all the other negative things that can drain you, pretty soon what you have is a limp, flaccid thing that cannot do what it's intended to do," I explain.

I draw my energy directly from the Sun each morning as I meditate and say my prayers, giving thanks to God for all life. I no longer request things from God, except to ask for the divine will to be done for all, while naming those I know with special needs. I feel that God already knows what I need so, instead of asking, I give thanks for all that has been provided me. Looking at the Earth as a living organism I feel that, as I pour out love to God in nature, God pours out love to me.

One of the most striking spiritual lessons I learned was at a conference where the Rev. Joseph Lowery, who worked closely alongside Dr. Martin Luther King Jr., told the audience,

"You know, everybody says 'God is on our side.' But God doesn't take sides. YOU better get on God's side, and the side of God is love."

Wow!! Words I live by.

****

CHAPTER SIXTEEN

In 2006 we fulfilled the promise we made in Yellowstone and took Frank Jr. and his wife June; their children Winston, Sydnee, Jordan and Taffrey, and Yero on a tour of Zion, Bryce and Grand Canyon National Parks. We flew into Las Vegas and rented an RV from a Black-owned company and spent nearly a week touring the parks. It was a heady experience to enjoy them vicariously through the eyes of the children who ranged from age four to sixteen. I can attest that there's no better way for a family to bond than being out in nature.

All the grandchildren wanted to help Frank cook on the campfire and, if the occasional bug fell in, he would tell them, "Oh, that's just more protein." When he had his shot of cognac in the evenings, he'd tell them it was to get rid of the phlegm in his throat. To this day we all still laugh about that, and the sight of the cousins bonding as they roasted marshmallows and made s'mores on the campfire is a pleasure I will carry in my heart forever.

To celebrate my 56th birthday and Frank's 70th we decided to go skydiving. We'd often talked about doing it and it felt like the right time. We drove from Atlanta to the airfield in Barnesville, Georgia, where a professional helped us suit up and gave us basic instructions. Each of us was flying tandem with the instructor on our back so it wasn't that risky, though we avoided telling our mothers.

When the plane got up to 14,000 feet and it was my turn to jump, I leapt out like a bird and screamed all the way down.

"Thank You, Jesus! Praise the Lord! Hallelujah!" I yelled at the top of my lungs.

The feeling of freedom and flying was so great! I was never a fearful person but, after that leap, all vestiges of fear left me.

The weather turned inclement shortly after I landed so we returned a few weeks later for Frank to enjoy his splendid jump. He had the same feeling of freedom.

One of the great things about Frank is that he always lets me believe that I'm the smart, talented one. It works until he's not around, and I suddenly find myself fumbling for the name of a bird, a date or a coherent explanation of something I'm trying to convey.

But the most dramatic example of our different abilities came one year when a couple of our friends decided to give him the opportunity to fly a glider on his birthday. He was ecstatic, and I was going to fly as well.

The young woman pilot took Frank up first, and he flew the plane like a pro. When they landed she gave glowing reviews of his ability and how she had let him put the plane into a stall so he could experience the momentary feeling of just hanging there. When she took me up she evidently assumed that I had roughly the same abilities, but when I put the plane into a stall it began nose-diving because I'd pressed the pedal so hard. The rest of the flight consisted of her trying to pull up and stabilize us. When we got to the ground her knuckles were white. Still, I'd been able to see the incredible views of the Tennessee Mountains for almost 300 degrees, so I was happy.

Another example of our difference that we fondly display in our apartment is a couple of wooden spoons that each one of us made while attending the same retreat at Knoll Farm in Vermont at different times. Each participant was encouraged to select a block of wood and carve a spoon from it. To look at Frank's, you'd think it was made by a craftsperson or a machine, while mine is a hunchbacked, misshapen thing ending in a sharp point. I tell myself it could serve in an emergency.

In November 2008, we learned from The Atlanta Tribune Magazine that we'd been chosen as a 2009 Power Couple. The magazine cited our work and provided another avenue for us to get the word out about the national parks and the plight of our environment.

Wherever I was asked to speak, I said yes. As a professional speaker I generally charge for each appearance, especially if it is to a White environmental group or corporate entity. If I'm asked to speak at a church or school which I know has a limited budget, I happily do it for free.

Once I was invited to speak at Adamsville Middle School in Atlanta. Thinking about what might interest children at that age, I decided to take the old buffalo tooth that Dr. Carolyn Raffensperger had found on her land in Idaho and given to me. I had a huge picture book with images of national parks, and I went to Underground Atlanta and bought a substantial amount of hard rock candy.

The teacher arranged for students from third, fourth and fifth grade to be in the auditorium, and I held them spellbound with stories and pictures. In particular I told them about the Buffalo Soldiers that protected the national parks and the giant 2,000 year old trees in Sequoia and Yosemite National Parks. I told them that those trees were so old, they were alive when Jesus was on Earth. Their eyes got so big. When I showed them pictures from Petrified Forest National Park where 75 million year old trees had turned to stone, their little mouths were literally hanging open. The rock candy and the old buffalo tooth were a big hit.

Later I received a packet of letters that their teacher had them write to thank me. They were hilarious. Almost all of them mentioned how much they enjoyed the rock candy and thanked me for bringing it. Several mentioned the Buffalo Soldiers and the buffalo tooth, and some were especially struck by the petrified trees. The ones that took the cake for me was from a young girl who told me, "You looked fabiless in that black dress," and the young boy who said he was going to go to college and finish his education so that he could become an environmentalist like me.

"It seemed like you were very interested to teach us," he ended.

Well, mission accomplished!

The night President Obama won the election in 2008, we were beside ourselves. Frank kept saying, "I just wish Dad was here to see this."

We lived just a few blocks away from Dr. Martin Luther King Jr.'s birth home, his father's old church, historic Ebenezer Baptist and the new Ebenezer, and the National Historical Park that bears his name. Most of historic Auburn Avenue District is maintained by the National Park Service, much like it was when Dr. King lived there as a child.

I knew that on this historic night the area would be teeming with people celebrating, so I jumped in the car and was there in about five minutes.

Sure enough there were crowds of people celebrating, still in disbelief. I went to the reflecting pool where Dr. King and Mrs. Coretta Scott King's casket float in the water, and paid tribute to the Eternal Flame that marks their lives. I was very conscious that Dr. King blazed the path that led us to this point and paid for it with his life.

The park is a treasure trove of places, artifacts and living history including the exquisite World Peace Rose Garden that Mrs. King planted. The Visitor Center contains the horse-drawn cart that carried Dr. King's body, and an exhibit of life-size sculptures of Dr. King and others leading a group of marchers, including a White man with one leg. Videos all around tell the story of Dr. King's life and share speeches that Civil Rights leaders gave.

Across the street in Dr. King's birth home you can see his bed and his toys just like when he was a child. The places where he and his siblings played hide and seek, the appliances in his parents' kitchen, and even the washing machine which they turned by hand, have all been preserved so that the public can understand his early life.

When people came to visit us it was the first place I took them. Once our friend Dr. Carolyn Finney's parents came to visit and she took them to the historic site. A former actress who'd backpacked around the world, she'd decided to go back to school early in the 21st century to study Environmental Geography. A Google search for African American environmentalists turned up our names, and she told me later how surprised she was that, when she sent me an email introducing herself, I sent her a rapturous response declaring that we were sisters. She's since completed her doctorate and we remain the best of friends and collaborators.

She brought her parents, Rose and Henry Finney, to dinner at our apartment that night and told us that in the middle of the tour, her dad suddenly grabbed her arm. Startled, she turned around and saw a look of terror on his face.

"What's wrong, Dad?" she asked in concern.

"We're not supposed to be in here," he said, pointing to a big black and white sign in the door, "Whites Only." It was only a display, an artifact of a bygone era, but for a moment her dad who had lived through that brutal time had slipped back through the veil and confronted the horror all over again.

It only lasted a moment, but Dr. Finney said she had never in her life seen her dad look so scared. She used that moment in her speeches, and so did I, to illustrate how the past is never really past, but alive in the experiences of many among us.

Frank and I decided that we had to be at President Obama's Inauguration ceremonies. We drove Big Red to DC and stayed with Iantha and her husband Kenny Wright in their spacious Fort Washington home. Early on Inauguration morning, Kenny drove us to the Metro station and we caught the packed train into DC. The mood was festive and it was almost like everyone had to pinch themselves to accept that it was real – America really had elected a Black man to the highest office in the land, and we would be there to see him installed. What a great day.

It was bitingly cold and everyone was on the Mall extra early to get a space. The love was so strong that, if you stepped on someone's foot, that person would beg your pardon. The entire day passed in a blur as we watched the President take the Oath of Office beside his elegant wife and beautiful young daughters. The crowd erupted when the precocious 8-year old flashed him a thumbs up! It felt as if our entire country deserved thumbs up that day.

Driving back to Florida we decided to take the Blue Ridge Parkway out of DC, and wind our leisurely way through the mountains. The parkway was established to preserve Appalachian mountain scenery and it was spectacular. Several times we came upon a "bear jam," meaning that someone spots a bear and everyone stops their car right where they are and gets out to catch a glimpse.

After a couple of hours' drive, we decided to get off and go back to Highway I-95. An hour later when we got down, we found that we had covered less than 100 miles in almost four hours. But it was worth it to us, and we did catch sight of a black bear on a hillside, feasting on berries.

In 2009, filmmaker and documentarian Ken Burns came to Atlanta on tour promoting his documentary series, *"The National Parks: America's Best Idea,"* which would be released later that year. I was looking forward to seeing how he'd treated the story of the Black Jones family who owned islands in Biscayne Bay, Florida beginning in 1897, and who were instrumental in the creation of Biscayne National Park. I had the opportunity to introduce the story to his partner, Dayton Duncan, at a formal dinner of the National Parks Conservation Association a few years earlier.

Knowing my passion to have the contributions of African Americans in the National Park System publicized, our friend Wally Cole, founder of Camp Denali and the North Face Lodge in Denali National Park, Alaska, arranged for me to be seated beside Mr. Duncan. He told me they were in the process of making a series about the national parks and wanted to include the contributions of non-White Americans. Straight away I told him the story of the Jones family.

The Black father, Lafayette "Pahson" Jones, had been enslaved, and after Emancipation made his way to Miami, where he used the sailing skills he'd learned to make a good living. He married a Bahamian woman, Mozelle, and they bought their first island, Porgy Key, in 1897 and moved there. They named their two sons King Arthur and Sir Lancelot after the Knights of the Round Table, programming them to accomplish great things.

And they did. Because in the 1970s Sir Lancelot stood up to developers and refused to sell his property to them, maintaining that people need places where they can go and be in the heart of nature. He eventually sold his island to the National Park Service which created Biscayne National Monument which later became Biscayne National Park, known today as the largest marine park in the entire system of almost 420 parks and historic sites.

Mr. Duncan was intrigued and sent me a note thanking me for being so kind and for engaging his 15-year-old son who was also at our table and a little out of place as one of very few young people in the room. When we published our first book in 2009, he sent me a lovely endorsement for the back cover.

Dr. Finney was contracted by our friend, marine archaeologist Brenda Lanzendorf, to research the Jones story. So I was agog to see what Mr. Burns had done with it.

On tour with him was our friend Ranger Shelton Johnson, the most famous park ranger in the country. Searching through the archives in Yosemite National Park, Ranger Johnson was the first to unearth the stories of the Buffalo Soldiers who protected the park in the early 1900s. His efforts to publicize them included inviting

Oprah to come up to the park, which she did with her friend Gayle King. He also wrote a fictionalized story, Gloryland, about these real-life heroes.

We'd met Ranger Johnson at a conference in Colorado in 1997 where we also met Dr. Dorceta Taylor, a prominent researcher on diversity and the environment. She was the keynote speaker and when I learned that she was Jamaican and grew up in Beckford Kraal just a few miles away from New Roads where I was born, I leapt over chairs to get to her when she finished speaking.

At the end of that conference, all the attendees were invited on a tour of Rocky Mountain National Park, and we drove high up to a meadow where we picnicked, while Ranger Shelton played his flute for us. Eeerie, haunting, and so beautiful. I imagined the souls who'd been in that place for eons gathering around to hear the purifying sounds.

The Ken Burns launch was held at the New Ebenezer Baptist Church, and I had the privilege of introducing him. From the dais I told the audience how happy and relieved I was because, now when I tell people about the amazing exploits of Black Americans that are preserved in the parks at the place where they happened, if they looked skeptical – which happens a lot – I could tell them to go check out Ken Burns' documentary. It's amazing how many White Americans need the corroboration of other White people to accept that something is true.

The greatest gift that came from that session was meeting Carolyn Hartfield, with whom I became instant best friends. The fitness expert who'd owned a natural vitamins store for years and who competed in Senior Olympics and I took to each other with a passion.

That year Frank and I were planning to hold a conference in Atlanta at which we would launch our new book, *Legacy On the Land: A Black Couple Discovers Our National Inheritance and Tells Why Every American Should Care*." We planned it for Sept. 23 - 26 and I set about raising the considerable amount of money it would require. I raised $90,000 to cover the costs of the conference space, plus travel and lodging for all our speakers and almost 100 young people from our friends' environmental programs around the country.

All the speakers waived their customary fees, including the inimitable MacArthur Genius Award winner Majora Carter; Queen Quet; Dr. Finney; Captain Bill Pinkney who sailed around the world by himself; Rue Mapp who was just launching her social media platform Outdoor Afro; and many others, including Kenn Stewart and the young underwater explorers he was training to become Master Divers; Jerry Bransford, descendant of the enslaved Black people who first plumbed the depths of Mammoth Cave National Park; and Darryl Perkins, a falconer who could call his bird out of the air to perch on his arm.

A large group of dedicated volunteers led by Carolyn Hartfield helped us plan the program and put everything together. Then it turned out that our dates coincided exactly with the time Frank needed to be in DC for the Congressional Black Caucus Annual Legislative Conference. Liaising with these members of Congress was a big part of his job. He was able to stay for the opening ceremonies keynoted by his Omega Psi Phi frat brother Robert Stanton, an African American who was Director of the National Park Service under President Bill Clinton.

The conference, "Breaking the Color Barrier in the Great American Outdoors," brought 250 people together, primarily environmentalists of color and the young people they served, as well as leaders of federal land management agencies and environmental allies. Many of the young leaders were meeting each other for the first time. We'd arranged tours to places such as Dr. Martin Luther King Jr. National Historical Park, and downtime, including a dance party, so people could really get to know each other. Many of today's most prominent young environmental leaders credit that conference for making a huge difference in their work.

One of the most celebrated participants in the conference and on the dance floor was Captain Pinkney, who made the voyage around the world when he was in his 50s because he wanted to show his grandchildren that you can do anything you set your mind to. He told us that sometimes when he was alone on the boat in the middle of the ocean, the stars were reflected in the water and he felt cradled between sea and sky, uncertain which was where.

The conference was a huge success. Many land management leaders who attended were shocked to meet so many Black, Hispanic and Asian people who were passionate about the outdoors and environment. They actually asked me, "Where did you find all these people?"

When it came time to settle the hotel bill, to my horror I was $3,000 short!!! What to do?

Thankfully I had long overcome my reluctance to ask for money. The discomfort I'd felt at going to my high school friends' home and asking to be paid for the fish their parents took on credit from Mama had left me very reluctant to ask for money, as I felt that somehow put me at a disadvantage.

The fact that my father brought me money only when he heard I'd done some extraordinary thing at school conditioned me to expect that I'd be given money when I did extraordinary things. But in the environmental field I was getting a lot of awards and very little money.

It wasn't until Iantha did a course in life coaching and gave me a free session that we walked back through my childhood and found out where I'd gotten hung up. And just like that, I was free!

So I called our friend Don Barry who'd recruited Frank to the Wilderness Society and was now Executive Vice President at Defenders of Wildlife. I told him my plight and he went to his President and persuaded her to sign off on a $3,000 investment to support the conference. Whew!

Not long after Director Stanton reached out and asked me to send him a list of some of the top leaders at the conference. Many of the people whose names I sent up were invited to President Obama's first White House Conference on America's Great Outdoors where the President told us how interested he was in helping make the public lands available to, and inclusive of, every American.

I was sitting in the second section and, though I could see him clearly, I wasn't close enough to shake his hand, though some of our colleagues including Rue and Queen Quet had that privilege. That's what you get for being a social butterfly running around talking to everybody instead of securing your spot, I learned. It was all good.

Frank vowed that when President Obama went to sub-Saharan Africa, we would be there. As a son of Mother Africa, he wanted to be there when a son of the race that had been torn away in chains returned wearing the highest crown. That's a 180-degree turn for you!

He scoured the papers and, on a Sunday morning when he saw in the New York Times that President Obama would be going to Ghana on a certain date, we booked our tickets that same day.

****

CHAPTER SEVENTEEN

Before we left the States we asked our friends if they knew anyone in Accra, and our friend Lurma Rackley told us her friend Dr. Erieka Bennett lived there. Arriving in Accra, deplaning and seeing the red earth and the greenery, Frank said it reminded him of the red clay land in Alabama where he was born. He said he felt like kneeling and kissing the ground. He'd finally come home to the Motherland.

We went straight to our hotel, The Golden Tulip, and it was exactly what we needed. It had the very important feature of a Tiki Bar where we could relax and enjoy a drink.

I felt just like I was in Jamaica. On the streets many of the women carried big loads balanced on their head, with a katta to cushion it, similar to what we used back home. I was surprised to see many children out selling things in the middle of the day, but I found out later that they go to school on rotation, some in the morning and some in the afternoon. In every way we felt welcome, as if we belonged there.

Dr. Bennett is a close friend and confidant of the President of Ghana and was closely involved in planning President Obama's state visit. We met her at the Diaspora Mission which she founded on property that includes the tomb of the great American philosopher, writer and trailblazer Dr. W.E. B. DuBois and Mrs.

DuBois. An elegant, beautiful, accomplished woman, Dr. Bennett welcomed us warmly. So did everyone in her office, which included a gift shop selling locally produced art and gifts.

She gave no sign of it then but, after we became close friends, she told us that she was very surprised when we showed up.

"When Lurma told me these noted environmentalists were coming to Ghana and I should take care of them, I assumed that you were White," she said. "Because the only Black environmentalist I know is my good friend Wangari Mathaai, the Nobel Prizewinner."

She went on, "I think what you are doing is really important, to reconnect African Americans with nature. We have neglected that side of ourselves. Since I've been with you, I find myself noticing the trees, I'm observing the birds, I'm noticing things that I just took for granted before. And it really makes me feel a deeper connection with the universe. It's making my life richer."

There were no tickets available for any events with President Obama, so we joined the throngs of people lining the highway and watched the motorcade go by. For the rest of our visit, Dr. Bennett introduced us to many of her friends and invited us to a party at her home. We remained steady friends and when she came to Atlanta a few years later to attend the birthday party of her trailblazing friend Mrs. Xernona Clayton, one of the first Black women in broadcasting, she invited us as well.

She was staying at a hotel in walking distance from our home. Speaking to her on the phone one evening she mentioned that she was just coming back from dinner with Lou.

"Which Lou?" I asked.

"Lou Gossett," she said. "We've been friends for many years."

Wow! So at the birthday party we got to meet not only the redoubtable Mrs. Clayton but also the actor Lou Gossett Jr. who was very gracious and embracing. We also met the legendary Cecily

Tyson, who was very elegant and somewhat aloof, and Chris Tucker, among many other celebrities.

One night we were sitting at the bar at our hotel in Accra and one of our favorite bartenders was on duty. Frank drinks Courvoisier and I drink red wine, and the bartender told Frank they were out of Courvoisier. I joked that he'd drunk the bar dry, but he often bought the bartenders a drink as well.

This night the bartender said to us,

"You know, I have three children, an 18-year-old son, a daughter who's six and a three-year-old boy. When my daughter saw how President Obama hugged his daughters she said to me, 'Daddy, why don't you ever hug us like that?' And it brought tears to my eyes."

"My grown son and I have never looked each other in the eye," he continued. "My father was not close to me so that's just how I thought it should be. But when my daughter said that, I almost broke down and cried. I hugged her and my three-year-old and I told them, from now on Daddy is going to hug you as much as you like."

Wow!! So we could see that lessons are taught not just with speeches and words but also in conduct. The gentleman was inspired to change his relationship with his children, just by observing President Obama's simple act of love. Who knows how many people in his circle will be affected by this change?

We had the choice of going to Cape Coast Castle on the ocean where untold numbers of Africans were held in beastly conditions before being shipped on the hellish journey to the New World, or going to Kakum National Park not far from it. Of course we chose the national park, because I refuse to expose myself to vicarious pain. There is nothing I can do to change the fate of my ancestors, and I didn't need to experience it to understand it.

Kakum National Park, on the other hand, was a joyful place of ancient trees and an intact forest. Our tour was led by a native ranger who told us that the greatest challenge was when herds of elephants came rampaging through, upending a lot of the trees. We walked on a rope bridge above the treetops and it was amusing to see some of the big strong-looking male visitors who put one foot on the ropes and absolutely refused to go any farther. I didn't blame them. We all have our challenges.

After the regular tour ended, we asked the ranger to take us on a personal tour. This is an experience I will never forget because, as he took us through the forest, he gave us a thorough lesson on the medicinal benefits of each tree. The leaves of this one are good for the stomach and digestion. The bark of that one is good for pain, and on and on.

It reminded us that medicines originally came from plants until man developed the technology to reproduce some of the elements from chemicals, and we see the results including deadly side effects. Frank and I often look at each other in wonderment and crack up laughing when we see the commercials in the U.S. that include, as a side effect, death. Wait, what?!

We lived in Atlanta seven blissful years, during which we got to meet and work with some of the country's top environmental leaders and also international stars. The Turner family were natural allies, and Laura Turner and her husband Rutherford Seydel invited us to events featuring cutting-edge environmentalists, such as Sir Robert Swan who was the first person to walk to both the North and South Poles. He is also the person who identified the hole in the ozone layer in the Antarctic, and had the color of his irises burned out as part of that trek.

We met Bill McKibben, the climate activist who founded the organization 350.0rg and publicized the need to keep carbon dioxide below 350 parts per million in the atmosphere before all hell would break loose. We met an author who exposed the lengths to which the fossil fuel industry had gone and was continuing to go in order to suppress technologies that produce renewable energy, citing Exxon Mobil in particular.

We met Ted Turner at a reception at his penthouse overlooking Centennial Olympic Park and the CNN building, and were gifted a signed copy of his autobiography. I learned two vital lessons from that book. The first is that the Secretary General of the United Nations said that when he and Ted walk down the streets of New York City, Ted will bend down and pick up trash and put it into garbage bins, with the observation that if everyone picks up some trash, soon there'll be none to pick up.

I took that to heart and though I won't pick up trash on the street, I deliberately pick up trash from the floor of public bathroom stalls and clean up after others to create the kind of space I want to come into.

The other thing that impressed me was a story Ted told about being on the Fastnet yacht race in Europe when a violent storm arose. He said his crew was very frightened and he told them, "Panic and you die." Fifteen people on other boats were killed. "Panic and you die" became an underlying mantra deep in my subconscious.

Laura also gave us tickets to sporting and entertainment events, so we got seats on the floor of Phillips Arena to see Shaquille O'Neal and Kobe Bryant play. I was so close that, if I stretched out my foot, I might trip them. She gave us tickets to rapper TI's farewell concert the night before he went off to jail. I'm sure we were the oldest people in the audience and sitting near the loud speakers was excruciating. We were glad for the experience, and left early. Rutherford invited me to serve on the Board of the Chattahoochee Riverkeeper, a venerable organization which I loved.

For several years Frank served on the Board of Visitors of the Nicholas School of Environment at Duke University in North Carolina. It's a beautiful campus with a gorgeous hotel overlooking the golf course. I loved going with him because it was a mini-vacation for me, just as when he came to Board meetings with me it was a mini-vacation for him. I could lie around and relax and watch movies while he went to meetings, and all I had to do was go down for lunch and receptions and sparkle and shine, which is my favorite thing.

One day when he came up at lunchtime Frank casually mentioned, "So Robert Redford is here and he's going to be at the reception tonight to pick up his award...."

Wait, what?

And he actually said, "I didn't tell you? Sorry!"

"No!! You didn't tell me!!" I'm sure I screamed.

I flew out of bed, got dressed and drove to the nearest mall. This called for a special outfit! I found a great little black dress and with my Native-made yellow bird feather earrings that I'd bought at Petroglyph National Park in New Mexico, I felt ready to meet Mr. Redford. The only person I've ever seen Frank excited to meet is President Obama.

The actor was there to pick up an award for his lifetime of leadership and environmentalism. I found him very gracious, humble and charming. When I had a chance to speak with him, I told him how there was a severe gap in the environmental sector when it came to people of color, and that more needed to be done to make people feel invited and included to participate.

He said, "Oh, environmental justice, like Majora Carter!"

Well, not exactly, but I'm always happy to be likened to Majora Carter, the Bronx environmentalist who stopped New York City from using her community as a dumpsite, and not only forced them to clean it up but persuaded Mayor Bloomberg to spend $1 million to help create a park on the waterfront where the dump had been. She went on to win the MacArthur Genius Award in 2006, with a prize of half a million dollars.

It was a great experience meeting Mr. Redford though, and I have a nice picture of us that immortalizes the moment.

One glaring contrast I saw between the White and Black organizations I served was the approach to money. I'd chuckle under my breath when a White organization with a multi-million dollar budget would get alarmed about the state of their fundraising and cash reserves. Meanwhile the Black organizations I served were lucky if we had $50,000 - $100,000 to work with for the year, and we accomplished so much with that, providing information and exposure to people who really needed the benefit of green in their lives.

The other amazing thing was how events and issues were compartmentalized. The week President Obama was elected, representing a seismic shift in American politics, I went to a Board meeting where it wasn't even mentioned. I waited for hours to see if someone would say something, and when it didn't happen I pointed out that this marked the demographic shift that had been projected for years, and showed that we needed to redouble our efforts to engage the Black and Brown population. You could have heard crickets chirping outside, the room got so quiet.

Shortly after a young White man entered the Emmanuel AME Church in Charleston, South Carolina and shot nine Black worshippers dead at point blank range in an act he told them was intended to exterminate the race, I attended a Board meeting about national parks. Again I waited the entire morning to hear that tragedy mentioned, especially since the church is part of the National Park System. Just before our first break, when I realized it apparently was not on anyone else's mind, I brought it up.

Again, people looked at me blankly as if to say, "What does that have to do with what we're here to talk about?"

In the environmental world the schism between place and people is the size of the Grand Canyon. Leaders get very concerned about protecting ecosystems and wildlife, but show very little interest in what happens to people. I found, and continue to find, this hugely disappointing. When we began working to raise the Black community's interest in the restoration of the Everglades our friend, environmental justice advocate Leola McCoy scoffed,

"Those people don't care about us. They only care about the birds and the bees and polar bears."

I thought she was wrong, but I came to find out she was right.

One of the great benefits of serving with organizations whose function is to advocate for the publicly-owned lands is that we get to visit so many national parks. Many Board meetings are held in national parks. At a meeting in the Grand Canyon, South Rim, I asked for a few minutes to address the full Board.

Standing in the center of the conference room at the historic El Tovar Hotel, with the canyon spreading out behind me and a roomful of White leaders including a couple of billionaires, I told them I found it a huge contradiction that we refer to the national parks as the "Soul of America," when in fact I never saw any of the people associated with "soul" in the parks. There was nobody who looked like Aretha Franklin or James Brown, and looking around one could easily believe that the parks had been purged of people of color.

I said that the demographic shift was upon us, and that we were effectively presiding over the demise of the Park System, if we did not speedily set about the business of engaging non-White people with the parks so that they'd come to love them and want to protect them.

"As more Americans of color are being elected to Congress, and Congress holds the purse strings to the parks' budget, why would they be inclined to appropriate millions of dollars for places that are as familiar to them as Mars? Why would they support places they don't know, that are unknown to their voters, when they have huge demands to fund housing, education and jobs which are more urgent priorities for their constituents?"

When I stepped down I saw Mike Finley, President of the Turner Foundation, smile at me and give an approving nod. And that was it. Business continued as usual.

Some years later, I was at a Board meeting in DC when the subject of privatizing the parks came up. I was adamantly opposed to the idea. Ken Burns pointed out in his documentary that, if the Park Service had not been established in 1916 to protect the parks, places like Grand Canyon would now be gated communities accessible only to the rich. I made it known that I found the idea entirely repugnant.

Then the chairman turned to me and said, "Well, what if the only way you can have Grand Canyon is if it's brought to you by a corporation?

"You can't bring me something I already own," I said, my eyes flashing daggers.

I think the other people at the table were stunned at my passion and directness. Others at the table joined in, and that conversation crashed and burned, for the moment.

One year we got to hike down into the Grand Canyon and spend the night. Just below the canyon rim we met a condor coming up. The largest flying bird with a wingspan of almost 10 feet from tip to tip, it rose effortlessly on the thermal currents in the canyon. It was fascinating to watch, and I thought about the numbers of these magnificent creatures that once inhabited the canyon. Today those numbers are severely reduced, though a breeding program is trying to bring them back.

It was a fairly easy hike 3,000 feet down to the midway point at Indian Gardens, where we would spend the night in the park rangers' dormitories. When we got there my colleagues decided to hike farther down to where they could see the Colorado River that chiseled this magnificent natural wonder of the world out of the colorful rocks over millions of years. I decided to stay by myself and enjoy the canyon solo. How many opportunities does a person get to do that, I reasoned.

I pulled a folding chair from a verandah and set it under the cottonwood trees. I could hear hikers going by on the trail but no one could see me. As I stretched out and closed my eyes, I felt as if every cell in my body was relaxing, every atom returning to its original perfection. I dissolved and floated away to join the canyon walls.

A ranger came by who was not in our party, and I have no idea how surprised or not he may have been to find a Black woman stretched out in his chair. He gave no indication, and asked if I wanted a glass of lemonade. Of course my answer was yes, and he went into his cabin and came out with two full ice-cold glasses. We may have sat there for an hour talking desultorily and solving all the problems on Earth, until members of my party returned, excited and exhausted.

As it got later, I saw what I consider a mating ritual very few people have seen or might interpret that way. The sun began to withdraw its rays from the canyon, starting at the bottom and slowly moving up the walls. It was as if a lover was undressing his lady for the night, raising her nightgown ever so gently. As the sun moved away, the moon sailed into view over the opposite wall and truly, I felt like I was in Heaven.

The park rangers made us a lovely spaghetti dinner and we had wine, so we went off to bed fully sated and uplifted. I was determined to wake up before dawn next morning to see the sunrise, and what an event that was. As the sun had undressed the cliffs the night before, in the morning it fully dressed them again. Its rays slowly and gently made their way down to the bottom of the canyon and lifted the darkness. That I will never forget.

Hiking back out of the canyon was much more challenging than it had been hiking down, and I was among the last of our group to get out. On the way down, the rangers had offered us beef jerky but I turned up my nose at it. It just didn't sound appealing. But on the hike back up, I happily indulged and it gave me the energy to get back over the rim.

✱✱✱✱

CHAPTER EIGHTEEN

In 2010 we were invited to present at the Aspen Institute/National Geographic Environment Forum where, at 8,000 feet above sea level, we felt as if were literally on top of the world. Many of the world's top climate, marine and atmospheric scientists were there, including Dr. Sylvia Earle. Known as "Her Deepness," she was the first woman to walk solo on the ocean floor, under a quarter mile of water. The actor Wendell Pierce, who was leading the effort to rebuild New Orleans after Hurricane Katrina, and actor Kevin Costner were among the luminaries speaking.

They warned that unequivocally we were heading over a cliff, and called for dramatic, immediate changes in American lifestyles and consumption patterns, if we are to maintain any semblance of an environment that can support human life. They said we had roughly 10 years to do it before we'd reach a stage of no return.

I was alarmed, and increasingly so because I did not see any momentum building to get the word to the masses, nor any indication that the system was gearing up to make the necessary changes. Frank and I said as much when we presented on a panel discussing racial diversity and inclusion.

We pointed out that obvious and basic steps that needed to be taken to engage African Americans and Latinos were still lacking – the majority of people still had no idea about the publicly owned lands system, and many of us who did, were still being made to feel as if we were an anomaly and not the norm. We said that, in light of the 10-year timeline they projected, it was vital that everyone lend their voices to push for more information and inclusion.

One of the most memorable moments came when I was sitting at a small group discussion table with Dr. Earle, the only person between us being oceanographer Dr. Andrea Neale, with whom I'd become instant best friends. As Dr. Earle described the condition of the oceans in graphic detail and what needed to be done, I suggested that we needed to find a simple way to persuade people how important our oceans are.

Dr. Earle turned to me, her eyes flashing, and asked,

"Do you like living here?"

"Yes, of course," I blubbered, unsure where she was going.

"Well, you cannot live on Planet Earth without oceans," she said. "The oceans are the engine of the environment."

Oops! Of course! That moment remains with me and I've used it many times to cut through clutter and get straight to the point. She also said that there's no such thing as "seafood."

"You're talking about marine wildlife," she said. "It wasn't just put there for our consumption on all-you-can-eat buffets."

I'll never forget that either, and we try to be mindful of what species are in decline, as that affects what we order when we eat out.

Returning to Atlanta was like coming back to Earth with a thud. In the face of so much urgency and so many compelling facts we'd just learned, back on the ground there was no urgency, no passion, and barely any attention to this "small detail."

Like Prometheus bringing fire, we brought the message back and pushed it out through our channels, including our blogs and newspaper articles, one of which I titled, "The Bizarre World I Live In," contrasting the heady discussion in Aspen to the inertia back in the cities. A handful of people wrote back to share their concern, but our relatively small platform barely made a dent when people saw weathermen and anchors on national TV networks treating climate change as a joke.

Frank's classmate and fraternity brother, nuclear physicist Dr. Walter Massey, was president of Morehouse College, and his former roommate Dr. Wilbur Leaphart was president of the Morehouse Alumni Association. Dr. Leaphart readily embraced our environmental activism and helped us get opportunities to speak on campus, as well as at Spelman College across the street.

When our book *Legacy on the Land* came out, our publicist got us interviews on the Tavis Smiley Show on National Public Radio; Rick Sanchez on CNN; Alex Witt on MSNBC TV; a feature in the Atlanta Journal Constitution, on local urban radio stations and a plethora of other media. Frank's friend and colleague at the Wilderness Society, Pat Byington in Alabama, helped us get TV interviews and book signings in Birmingham.

We became as well known in Atlanta as we were in Fort Lauderdale. We were honored as Pioneers by the Auburn Avenue Research Library, and outdoor recreation became a part of the Annual Sweet Auburn Festival for the first time. Our partner REI (Recreation Equipment Incorporated) sponsored a pavilion that included our friends Angelou and James Ezeilo, founders of Greening Youth Foundation, and Nadine Patrice, founder of Operation Green Leaves Haiti.

The single most memorable event from that period was when our friends at Delaware North invited Frank and me to serve as Visiting Squire and Lady of the Bracebridge Dinner, an annual celebration depicting the magical Manor Hall of author Washington Irving's Squire Bracebridge. The celebration described as one of America's best loved holiday traditions was directed by the artist Ansel Adams for many years, and went on for several days over

Christmas. Hundreds of people came dressed in their finery, and the Squire and Lady were the titular hosts.

Dressed in our fine costumes that had been worn by many other Squires and Ladies before, we were leading the procession onto the dais at the Ahwahnee Hotel when one of my high heels got caught in a crack in the steps. I hesitated for a moment and whispered to Frank telling him what was happening.

"Just keep moving, Babe. Just keep moving," he whispered back.

So I took my foot out of the shoe and walked the remaining few steps, my bare foot invisible under the long gown. After we sat down at the table enjoying the opulent seven-course meal and the performance, including trumpeting angels, I felt someone gently slip the shoe on my foot under the table.

"Just keep moving, Babe," became another mantra to me, my other one being, "When the going gets tough, Audrey is outta here."

The Wilderness Society decided to close the Atlanta office at the end of 2010, and we were ready to go back to Fort Lauderdale and fulfill one of Frank's longest-held dreams. He told me that, as a little boy driving in the car with his dad across the bridge in Fort Lauderdale and seeing the sailboats on the water below, he'd dreamt that one day when he grew up he'd buy a sailboat and go sailing around the world.

In preparation for this adventure, we went to the Virgin Islands in 2006 with the annual Black Boaters Summit and learned to sail, each of us getting our captain's license to sail in coastal waters. The BBS, as it is commonly called, was the brainchild of Captain Paul Mixon, and one of its stars was Captain Pinkney.

When we arrived in St. Thomas, we were walking on the dock when we ran into Dru Stafford, one of Frank's friends from Howard University. They hadn't seen each other in more than 50 years and had a happy reunion. She was also part of our group learning to sail.

I have a voracious appetite so, in this exciting new country, I ate practically everything I saw. When we got onboard the 54-foot Beneteau that would be our home for the next three weeks, two big things happened.

First, our Captain called Frank and said, "Take her out."

Say what? BBS had sent us manuals to study and CDs to watch, but I expected that when we got to St. Thomas we would be taking classes and getting more training.

Frank, completely surprised and never before handling a luxury yacht, stepped up and took the helm. It was moored among many other luxury boats, creating the potential for a very expensive accident. He was masterful and soon we were out of the port and in open water. I know he surprised himself and he definitely surprised me.

The second thing that happened was I got violently ill. My stomach felt like it was on a roller coaster. I told the group that I had just eaten too much of everything and all I needed was to go below deck and sleep it off.

I saw Frank looking so crestfallen, as if resigning himself to the end of his dream. If I was going to be perpetually seasick, it would be very difficult for us to live the sailing life. As I expected, after a nap I was right as rain. Frank was so relieved.

Frank had been searching the internet for years looking for the right boat. He'd even thought about going back to Holland to buy one he saw for sale, but the price of transporting it and the taxes were prohibitive. Just before we left Atlanta he found a boat he loved in, of all places, Hollywood, next door to his hometown Dania.

Moving back to Florida was a joyful experience. We had lots of friends and family there, although Frank's mom had passed on some years earlier at age 90. A few weeks after her birthday our niece had called and told us that Mom said she was tired and ready to go. Dad had been gone for more than 10 years and she continued to live in the house on the lake that they'd shared for over 50 years.

She used to tell us that if she felt a pain in the night she'd get out of bed, walk into the bathroom, throw her medicine cabinet door open and say to the pain,

"See? I don't have anything for you. I don't have anything to rub you or massage you or take care of you. You better go find somebody that can help you."

She died within a month from no apparent illness, when just she and Frank were in the house. I'd taken a break to go to the beach, and before I got there he called and told me she was gone. Though we mourned her passing, we were encouraged that she had lived such a great and God-centered life, and she had apparently even died on her own terms.

Back in Fort Lauderdale we stayed with our longtime friends Lee Hainline and Jim Cross. As soon as we unpacked and put our things in storage, we headed out to look at the boat.

At first I wasn't impressed. She was big – 43 feet in length, 13 feet across with an 83-foot mast. A motor sailor with a powerful engine, she carried 600 gallons of diesel fuel and 300 gallons of water. She had a lot of teak which needed to be refinished, but she had the one thing I'd told Frank was indispensable to me – an indoor wheelhouse. If we were out in inclement weather, I wanted to be sheltered below deck and still be able to steer the boat.

When I saw the look of joy on Frank's face, that sealed it. After taking her on a shakedown cruise, we bought her cash and turned her over to an outfitter to make necessary improvements, including refinishing the teak.

They say that BOAT means Break Out Another Thousand, and that became painfully true when we got back from Holland where we'd gone to the wedding of Braddie and Marion's son Alex, and the outfitter handed us the bill. But we could cover it and our approach is - what's money for, if not to help you do what you want?

Though Frank retired from his formal job, we kept our consulting business going and both of us wrote prolifically as a community service. For years I had a blog published in the Huffington Post every couple of weeks and also sent it out to our list of approximately 5,000 people. Frank wrote about the environment from his unique perspective of someone who grew up in the area and had seen the changes over 70 years, and the publishers of The Westside Gazette and the South Florida Times newspapers carried our stories regularly.

I also had opinion pieces published in The Hill newspaper that covers Congress. We got requests for interviews from all over the country and our perspectives are included in multiple dissertations, at least five books and scores of magazines. We were a key part of the engine of a network of Black and Brown environmentalists and outdoor advocates growing across the nation.

CHAPTER NINETEEN

We moved aboard our boat in September, 2011 and docked her at a slip in the Fort Lauderdale City Marina. By a strange twist of fortune, we were a stone's throw from the bridge crossing the span that Frank and his dad had driven over when he first got the idea to be a sailor.

The boat was a sturdy Cheoy Lee built in China in the 1980s. Our outfitter said the hull was so thick that, if we ran into anything, we wouldn't have to worry about her, as the damage would be done to whatever we struck. Of course we had no intention of striking anything, thank you very much.

Her name was the Wu-Wei – loosely translated as "doing effortlessly." That was certainly our preferred way of doing things – going with the flow – but it was quite disconcerting when we took her out to sea. We had to radio the bridge tenders who raise and lower the bridges over the New River and the Intracoastal Waterway. When we asked for an opening for the Wu-Wei, they invariably responded that they were opening for the "Wee Wee."

Well, we were not going to be the Wee Wee, so we decided to break with tradition and change her name. Apparently among sailors there's great reluctance to change a boat's name for fear it will bring bad luck. We settled on the name "Limitless," and so she was rechristened.

She was so spacious that it was like living in a small condominium. In the V-berth master cabin we had a huge bed that could comfortably sleep four people. It had built-in shelves on two sides above the bed where we stored books and the things we used regularly. Drawers built into the platform bed and a space under the mattress provided extra storage.

A few steps from our bed was the bathroom where we had a sink, toilet and shower. We chose to use the bathroom facilities in the marina in order to cut down on the number of times we had to do a "pump out." This involved attaching a machine with a hose to the outlet and connecting it to the city's sewer system. It was usually Frank's job, though I helped "supervise." With the addition of our flat screen TV connected to cable, we had all the comforts of home.

Two steps up from our bedroom, we entered the salon which included the kitchen and living area. A propane stove with an oven, a built-in refrigerator and freezer, a dining table surrounded by a sectional couch and a satisfactory amount of counter space made cooking and entertaining quite comfortable. I could whip up a meal of oxtails, rice and peas, curry chicken or chicken soup – all our Jamaican favorites – in no time.

Three steps up from the salon was the pilot house, with a helm, the Captain's chair that seated two, and a large counter space that held things we used regularly, such as books, CB radio and binoculars. In the rear, four steps down from the pilot house, were two aft cabins, one that could sleep two and the other that slept one. A bathroom with sink, shower and toilet served both cabins.

The dining room table could be raised or lowered, and with the addition of a custom-made cushion that fit over it we could comfortably sleep seven people on board. We had a flat screen TV in the salon, so everyone could be comfy. We even had a washing machine on board, though we never used it.

We expected that when we went sailing we'd have our friends, longtime sailors Kim and Jim Anaston-Karas with us as our co-captains. She's a slender, beautiful 5-foot blonde while he is about

6-foot-four inches tall and very buff. We had enough space to be at sea together for a while without feeling cramped.

Most nights we left the hatch open until around midnight when Frank went up and closed it. We never felt in any jeopardy, and security guards patrolled the docks at night. It was also a favorite place for the City police to come and meet each other. Besides, boating in Fort Lauderdale is a multi-billion dollar industry, so the authorities are very careful to take care of boaters.

Still, Frank kept a small axe and his Bowie knife on his side of the bed. We also had a golf club nearby that I was awarded by the Fort Lauderdale Links, in case we had to defend against an intruder.

A Publix supermarket was a 10-minute walk across the bridge and we were surrounded by really good restaurants, my preferred being The Chimney House, a Cuban restaurant a block away. My favorite meal there was the grilled salmon with rice and grilled veggies, with a glass of cabernet followed by their superb flan.

It got to the point where the waitresses at the Chimney House would smile when they saw us come in and tell me what I was going to have. Usually I don't like being predictable, but this was worth it. I'd always wanted a place like on the TV sitcom "Cheers," where everybody knows your name, and here we had it.

Whenever friends came to visit, we'd take them to the Chimney House or the Briny Pub, an Irish restaurant and bar down the dock, where we could get fish and chips and ice cold beer.

The marina was in a city park, and we were directly in front of a cabana with benches and two long tables. People – mostly White – drove up and parked in the metered parking lot to sit at the tables and enjoy the incredible views. The Riverwalk Trail ran in front of our boat and ended a few slips west. It went a little over a mile east and emptied into Las Olas Boulevard, the Rodeo Drive of Fort Lauderdale.

We could walk from the boat along the trail to Las Olas and continue along the pricey boulevard to Fort Lauderdale Beach about two miles away. Every first Sunday there was a free jazz concert at the pavilion just down the Riverwalk Trail across from the Discovery Museum, and whatever activities were happening downtown we had a prime seat.

We could walk to everything. The Broward Performing Arts Center was in our front yard, so we could dress up and walk to events and walk back at night with no concerns at all. At Christmastime transient boaters were asked to leave the marina to make space for boats coming in to participate in the Annual Christmas Parade. We enjoyed the festively decorated boats passing by us early evening, before we walked down to where the parade started at nightfall.

At first, it seemed that nobody – Black or White – could believe some Black people owned a sailboat. Seeing Frank in the marina bathroom which also included the laundry room, several White men asked him if he had a boat in the marina. The answer should have been self-evident because you had to have a code to get in, and only people who lived or worked there would have the code. Frank good-naturedly said, "Yes. Slip 10."

Fortunately I didn't get the same questions from women in the ladies room and, once people knew we were boaters, they were very friendly and welcoming. Several couples invited us over to their boat for drinks and dinner, and we made some lifelong friends. I was surprised to find how many of the men were retired pilots. I guess it takes similar skills to fly as it does to sail.

The first week we were there, everyone got together in the cabana for a "Sundowner" bringing drinks and something to eat that we all shared. (When I mentioned at a Board meeting that we were buying a boat and planning to live aboard, a young man told me how some friends of his had done that and become alcoholics, so they had to give it up and go to Alcoholics Anonymous. I assured him we did not have that worry.)

Our marina was on the route of the Jungle Queen Tour Boat which went by six times every day forward and back, at 10 a.m., noon, and at 2, 4, 6, and 9 p.m. for the dinner cruise. I'm sure we appear on hundreds of people's videos because people literally were agog to see us.

In the first few years we were on deck a lot when the boat passed, and sometimes I deliberately ran up from below deck when I heard the announcer's voice marking its approach. By the dinner cruise at 6 p.m. Frank would usually be on deck having his evening cognac while I had a glass of cabernet.

The expression on some faces was priceless. People would actually point at us and nudge each other. Many Black people seemed overjoyed and waved deliriously. Some stared straight ahead as if we were a personal affront. Children in particular were delighted to see us, and I was never as happy as when I saw a boatload of Black schoolchildren going by and waving excitedly.

"Yes, you can have a boat and go sailing around the world if you want," was my unspoken message, expanding Frank's experience as a child.

People in the cabana repeatedly asked us if that was our boat. I don't know if they ever asked the people on either side of us that question. Once we saw a Black couple sitting at the picnic table. Frank was on his way to the facilities when the gentleman called out to him, "Excuse me sir! Is that your boat?"

When Frank said yes he turned back to the lady and shouted excitedly, "I told you it was their boat!"

Since there were only two boats between us and the place where people launched their motor boats and canoes into the water, we were very visible and caused a lot of double takes. Like, "What, did I really see a Black person on that boat? And they own it? What is the world coming to?" We had many good laughs imagining those conversations.

When we took her out, Limitless handled like a champ. We motored out with the sails still furled, passing under the 4th Street bridge, the Andrews Avenue Bridge and gliding down Millionaire's Row where every house was a mansion. We don't necessarily have a lot of respect for lavish displays of wealth. Still, they were gorgeous and many had spectacular landscaping that, opening up on the expanse of the Intracoastal Waterway, made them eye-popping.

When we got under the 17th Street Causeway at Port Everglades where the cruise ships docked, and navigated the narrow Governor's Cut that connected the Intracoastal and the Atlantic, we were free. Then we could unfurl the sails and let her rip. Frank could be at the helm steering by the compass while I relaxed, or vice versa. Kim and Jim were with us, which really helped my sense of safety.

Once we went out when the weather report called for four-foot seas, but the wind picked up and the Atlantic was much rougher than predicted. Limitless dipped and bucked and rose up as if to say, "This is what I was made for!" She showed that she could handle rough seas with aplomb.

It was exhilarating and freeing to be on the water. All we could hear was the sound of the wind in the sails and the water parting as the boat ploughed through.

Shortly after we moved on board, we realized it wouldn't be that easy to live aboard and go sailing. Before going out we had to put away all the things we use - imagine packing up your condo or apartment to go on a day trip and unpacking it all when you get back.

The marina was known as a hurricane hole, meaning it was fairly safe in a hurricane. Our plan was to be there from September to the end of the hurricane season in November, after which we'd take off for Jamaica and parts unknown. The boat held so much fuel and water that we could easily be out for a couple of weeks without having to pull into a port. Just like we'd gone around the country, we planned to keep our itinerary loose and go wherever our desire and the weather took us.

When a hurricane approached, Frank would watch how the wildlife behaved to help decide whether it would hit or not. If the ducks were just calmly going about their business, he'd feel fairly sure that we were not in jeopardy. In 1992 when Hurricane Andrew hit, we'd noticed all the ducks taking off in a hurry.

But, if the warnings got strident, we'd decide that caution was the better part of valor, take down the main sail, adjust the lines to give the boat maximum ability to ride the waves, and go stay with our friends Lee and Jimmy in suburbia. They actually had hurricane sheeting made from Kevlar, and after we put it up we could comfortably relax on their wrap-around patio and watch the storm unleash its power outside.

As soon as the threat was over, we'd hurry back to the boat to make sure she was OK. In the hurricane of 2018, we found that a huge ornamental palm tree about 60 feet tall and twelve feet around blew down, but thankfully it fell to the west. If it had fallen to the south it would have taken out Limitless and the two boats to port and starboard. Our gratitude was unspeakable.

✸✸✸✸

CHAPTER TWENTY

My mother's health had been declining for some time, and shortly after we bought our boat it suddenly took a nose dive. She and Ruth Williams, her longtime friend from Jamaica since they worked at Seprod, had moved from New York and shared Ruth's house in Kissimmee near Orlando. Her illness meant that I was on call at all times. It was a three-hour drive from the boat to her place door to door, and Frank and I made the journey many weekdays and weekends.

I found that I needed to be her advocate because, although she was very intelligent and feisty, she was convinced that many people in the medical field dismissed her for the three cardinal sins of being Black, overweight and old. I was determined to stand in the gap for her. She called me her pit bull after I had to go toe to toe with her doctors a couple of times.

Year after eventful year passed while we lived at the marina. We didn't go very far, but the world came to us.

Once we had an artist to starboard and a PhD educator and former pilot to port. Julia Newhouse the artist created exquisite designs on leaves from the sea grape tree and gave me one of those beautiful treasures. She and her husband Dennis Jay came in periodically on their way from their homeport Annapolis to and from the Caribbean. The educator Ellen King wrote books and we had spirited conversations with her and her husband Jerry who'd flown for Pan Am. They came in from a stint sailing in Turkey and stayed for a while. We went out to dinner together many times. Thankfully we shared the same ideas about politics and what our country should represent.

Ann Robertson and her husband Bill had us over for drinks and a sumptuous dinner on their boat and we remain in close touch, as we do with Ingrid DuLac Tower and Keith and Katrina Greenwood. A wonderful couple, Rick and Mary Reich, drove down from Pennsylvania every year after Thanksgiving and took a slip for several months. I felt especially lucky when they got a slip near us because Mary was an incredible baker. Some mornings as soon as we woke up she'd be knocking on the hull holding hot scones or some exotic baked goods. She made enough to give some to everyone in the 30-boat marina.

Wildlife in the marina was very plentiful and varied. Families of Muscovy ducks roamed around and it was the cutest thing to see a family of fluffy yellow newborn ducklings waddling behind a mom. At some point the mother would take the little ones onto the dock and jump off to show them how it was done. Just like children, some would leap right off and begin paddling while others hung back and had to be persuaded by mom's insistent quacks.

Frank's one beef was that people came to the marina with bread and fed it to the ducks, resulting in an unholy mess. He was very firm in telling people not to feed them in front of our boat.

"Ducks are carnivores," he said. "Their diet is worms and things that they pull out of the earth."

There were always flocks of Ibis in the parking lot, and a resident Little Green Back Heron that we saw a lot. A couple of Yellow-crowned Night Herons came by regularly, along with the occasional Great Blue Heron. One morning I walked into the salon and looked through the window preparing to go up on deck, and saw a Great Blue Heron sleeping on the piling where our lines were tied up. Wow!!! I have a passion for capturing every wild moment, but I wasn't able to get that picture. Frank took multiple photos of a Great Heron and the Little Green Backed Heron perched on our lines.

The river was rich with life, although we would never eat anything from that water which no doubt had excessive amounts of diesel fuel from all the boats. A couple of Black men crabbed off the end of the pier west of us. I went down and talked with them and they told me they'd been crabbing there for years. Once I saw the process of catching crabs - putting a chicken leg in a metal trap and lowering it into the water, I wasn't so hot on eating crabs anymore.

One day I was sitting on deck talking on the phone with Iantha when I heard a big splash behind me. I turned around just in time to see a huge sting ray leaping out of the water and back, its white belly and gray body ending in a long spiny tail visible for just a moment. Wow! What a gift!

Beginning in November we saw manatees go by in large groups, coming down from the north where it was getting colder. One New Year's Day Frank and our close friend Al Calloway, a leader of the Student Nonviolent Coordinating Committee (SNCC) which was instrumental in the success of the Civil Rights Movement, were sitting on deck having a few drinks and talking when they counted 100 manatees go by. At that point they stopped counting. Al lives just across the river from us and could see our boat from his penthouse. Whenever we were out of town he'd go by periodically to check on Limitless.

One early morning I went out and saw a manatee near shore, apparently fast asleep. It was so close I could touch it. I restrained myself with great effort and took a picture. It woke up, turned its huge unwieldy body around – it's called a sea cow for a reason – and went back out into the river. I was able to get a video of the whole thing. Wow!

The New River leads from the Intracoastal Waterway near the Atlantic Ocean and the North Fork of the river runs through the heart of the historically Black community called Sistrunk. Legend has it that the Native Americans say the river was not always there, that one night they were woken up by a tremendous bang, and next morning there it was.

Living aboard our boat satisfied my desire to be out in nature, because you can't get much closer than that. I'd wake up in the morning to the sounds of wild parrots squawking as they flew in large flocks from the Live Oak trees across the river where they roosted. I'd bounce out of bed leaving Frank still asleep, walk up two steps to the salon where I'd put on the coffee, walk up three more steps to the wheelhouse and then five more up on deck.

Nearly every morning I'd take a picture of the sun the first time I saw it rising over the Atlantic and post it on Facebook with a note of gratitude. Then I'd settle down on deck with coffee and meditation books and call Iantha, my meditation partner since 1997.

Iantha was instrumental in my spiritual growth. She'd been a vegetarian for more than 20 years when we met, and had a very spiritual, though non-religious, approach to life. In one of our early sessions I said something about feeling like I'd died and gone to Heaven.

"Oh Audrey," she said gently. "The idea is to LIVE as if you're in Heaven."

And that became another mantra. I had seen Heaven on Earth. I went to bed at night being rocked gently on the water, and sometimes more energetically when a speedboat went by. Many times when we were off the boat in a hotel or other bed we'd suddenly get the rocking feeling deep inside, a most soothing feeling. I could also see the moon and the stars through the hatch over our bed.

And soon I began to see the ominous signs of climate change and sea level rise all around us. Across the river, a few hundred yards away, a residential neighborhood backed up to the water. When the tide came in at the full moon, it washed right over the sea wall and spilled into their backyards. On our end it raised our boat almost as high as the dock, and flooded the parking lot for 50 yards. Sometimes I had to pretend to be a ballerina, stretching my legs four feet or so to touch the deck or the dock getting on or off the boat.

In 2012 I was invited to debut my second book at the Badlands Astronomy Festival in Badlands National Park by my young friend Tricia Smedley, who I met while serving on the Board of the Association of Partners for Public Lands. She told me that my great hero, astronaut Dr. Story Musgrave, would be the keynote speaker, and she would book me into the bed and breakfast where he was staying so I might have a chance to spend some time with him. Oh joy!

I had fallen in love with Dr. Musgrave when I first read about him performing "eye surgery" on the Hubble Telescope in outer space. When the telescope was launched in 1992 and began to send the first pictures from space back to Earth, scientists were extremely disappointed that all the pictures were blurred. By some great misfortune, the lenses were not properly aligned.

Dr. Musgrave was selected to fix them. I have a picture of him in his bulky space suit hanging off the end of the space station, working blindly to try and fix the lens. He had no idea if what he did was a success until later when the first pictures came back and voila! They were absolutely perfect and unearthly in what they revealed.

As a stargazer Dr. Musgrave loomed large in my imagination. I was going solo to this conference, and I often thought about what I might say when I met the great man. I just hoped I didn't dissolve into a puddle and start stuttering.

I drove through the phantasmagoric landscape of Badlands National Park where just two years earlier a ten-year-old girl picked up a fossil right outside the Visitor Center that turned out to be part of a rare, well-preserved saber tooth that was millions of years old. My lodging sat at the top of a hill with a vast expanse of the park visible for 200 degrees around.

As I walked into the lobby a woman was coming up the stairs and went behind the desk. Approaching her, I saw none other than my icon turn the corner into the room. I'm sure my eyes popped. The receptionist said, "Oh, Dr. Musgrave! I hear your wife is with you?"

"Yes," he said. "She's round the corner with our daughter."

Just then a gorgeous young brunette put her head around the wall. I was about to say, "Wow! Your daughter is so beautiful," when suddenly Frank appeared on my shoulder.

"Honey," he cautioned, "do not assume anything about people's relationships."

He'd also suggested that I stop telling people how much they look like other people because they might not always find that pleasing.

I thank God forever that I never uttered those words, because just then Dr. Musgrave said,

"Oh, here's my wife and my daughter now," as the young woman came into the room with a young girl about seven years old following behind her.

Whew! That was close! Dr. Musgrave was in his mid-70s and his wife looked to be about 30.

I feel certain we would not have had the relationship we enjoyed that weekend if I'd made that blunder. We hit it off right away, and as his wife and daughter were often out playing, we wound up seated together lingering over breakfast in this breathtaking place. I know I must have been making some sense, but for the life of me I have no recollection what we talked about.

The second night of the festival when Dr. Musgrave was scheduled to speak, I joined a crowd of about 400 people seated in the outdoor amphitheater surrounded by towering, jagged peaks. It was dusk when he started speaking and we began to see the first stars popping out. Taking the stage Dr. Musgrave traced his destiny to fix the Hubble in extreme conditions in space back to his childhood and his curiosity about how things work.

He said that, growing up on a farm in Massachusetts, he learned to drive all the machinery by the time he was five, and could fix them by the time he was seven. He said his mother allowed him to go out alone at night into the pine forest around the farm, and he taught himself how to tell direction by his fingertips. He memorized the feel of the bark on the side of the trees as he entered so he could follow it back out in the dark. That early training was instrumental in his ability to fix the Hubble as he literally had to fumble for the parts, hanging off a robotic arm, working in a bulky space suit outside the Earth.

Dr. Musgrave warned that this is the first time in recorded history that human beings are drawing the majority of our information from "content" developed by other humans on TV and on our hand-held devices, with little connection to nature. He reminded us that we are creatures of Earth and Cosmos, and we need to live in balance with both.

Sitting there we could see the Milky Way Galaxy extending like a gigantic necklace above us. I almost wept with joy, so great was the feeling of belonging to a benevolent universe. I lost count of how many shooting stars I saw. As the great astronomer used his laser pointer to stroke the dark skies and identify planets, constellations and individual stars, the Space Station suddenly came into view, passing silently overhead. A collective whoosh of breath escaped from the audience and Dr. Musgrave chuckled in delight, remembering his time on it.

I cannot overstate how pivotal that moment was for me. I've had opportunity to speak to thousands of people across the United States since, including many young people just starting their careers. I like to start out with an image from the park taken that night by a professional, of the Milky Way seeming to stream out of a hole in one of the giant earthen walls of the park. I remind them that Earth is one of eight (used to be nine until Pluto was demoted) planets in a very small solar system on the very edges of the Milky Way Galaxy which itself is like a grain of sand on a beach of galaxies in space.

I point out that none of us knows how we got here, and none of us knows how or when we will leave – some people who've tried to end their lives wind up having to live with devastating deformities. Then I remind them that all the ways that humanity has found to differentiate ourselves from each other, such as "race," are artificial, contrived to benefit one group of people at the expense of another. I tell them that, if we accept that God evolved us all here, then everything that is here must also belong to all of us.

I'm always encouraged by how enthusiastically the audience responds when I tell them that, since we made up all these differences, we can agree to discard them now that we see how poorly they serve us. People often erupt in a standing ovation at the end, because they've never thought about it that way.

CHAPTER TWENTY-ONE

The drumbeat about climate change and sea level rise was steadily increasing, and everywhere we went along the riverfront we could see it with our own eyes. Even with a modest rainfall, the streets were flooded and water was coming UP through the storm drains. A minor storm pushed so much sand onto the roadway that Fort Lauderdale Beach along A1A, the strip famous for Spring Break revelry, was closed for days.

To our astonishment, building continued unabated right along the seashore and the riverfront. We drove downtown Miami and Brickell Avenue, where Frank used to have his offices in the Audubon office on the Miami River, and found that there are places where you can no longer see the sun. Nor can you see Biscayne Bay, which was a major attraction.

Years earlier we'd collaborated on a White Paper with Audubon titled, "In South Florida the Environment is the Economy," showing how we need to protect the environment if we are to continue to have a thriving economy. Millions of tourists come from all over the world to enjoy the sunshine, the beaches and the vibe of the area. Now we could see that the caution had not been heeded because the building boom was cannibalizing the environment, and pollution has led to annual episodes of "red tide" which decimate sea life and make some of our beaches rank and uninviting.

Frank kept marveling, "How are the insurance companies continuing to insure places that are going to be underwater in 30 years?"

We soon found out that Florida is the state with the highest value of property covered by the National Flood Insurance Program, three times as much as the next highest state, Texas. So in the event of a disaster, the wealthy people behind the developments will cash out first, potentially bankrupting the insurance for people of lesser means. Of course we wrote about that.

One of my proudest moments was when our friend Kate Cell, Climate Campaign Manager at the Union of Concerned Scientists (USA) engaged our company to review a report they were preparing, "Surviving and Thriving in the Face of Rising Seas." The report paid particular attention to communities of color and low-income communities that are most vulnerable to the effects of climate change, and laid out a plan for what needs to be done to prepare them and to help them cope. She also engaged us to review their work on "National Landmarks at Risk," looking at how some units of the National Park System were being affected by rising seas.

I could write volumes about Kate, whom I often hold up as a shining example of a non-racist. In our first conversation she said – as many people do – something about calling to "pick my brain." I told her firmly that I don't allow people to pick my brain because that's the same as picking my pocket.

"Our intellectual capital and our experience is how we make our living," I told her.

She got it immediately, apologized, and has been using that statement for years to encourage her colleagues not only to engage environmental professionals of color but also to be prepared to pay for our expertise. Kate's husband Sean works to reduce the threat of nuclear war, and contracted with Earthwise to help inform the Black community and Congressmen and women about the urgent need for Congress to take back its power to declare war. That power was ceded to the President after the attack of 9/11, and Congresswoman Barbara Lee and Congressman Ted Lieu have been out front striving to reverse that. We met with Congresswoman Lee on Capitol Hill to continue that dialogue.

I especially appreciate Kate's readiness to pay for services. It's a carefully constructed myth that salaries are low in the environmental sector, although many of the top leaders easily make half a million dollars or more a year in salary and benefits. Sadly they will complain that they have no money to pay professionals of color who are in far more tenuous financial position. When people call to engage members of the Speakers Bureau we formed in 2014, one of the first things I ask besides the subject matter and date is, What's your budget? I find little value in investing my time in a conversation that will go nowhere because we don't work for free. "It takes dollars to make change," I say.

Many times I felt like a voice crying in the wilderness. The signs of a looming climate crisis were all around us, but the majority of people just couldn't see. Or maybe they felt powerless to help change anything. It did not help that the governor of Florida was a climate denier who forbade state workers from using the term climate change. Considering that, in every study, South Florida, and particularly the areas of Miami Beach and the coastline including Hollywood, Dania, and Fort Lauderdale, were in the bull's eye, literally Ground Zero for impacts from sea level rise, this attitude was just incomprehensible.

Congressman Hastings, whose district included many of these places, was our staunchest advocate. For multiple years he sponsored us to present a session at the Congressional Black Caucus' Annual Legislative Conference, where we informed people from all over the country about the national parks and forests and the emerging climate crisis.

One year he invited me to come to Capitol Hill and testify to members of a Natural Resources committee about the status of the Everglades restoration and its effect on the Black community. The presenters that day, besides me, included Shannon Estenoz,

Executive Director of the South Florida Ecosystem Restoration Task Force; Craig Obey, Legislative Director of the National Parks Conservation Association; and Dr. Tom Van Lent, Vice President of Science and Education at the Everglades Foundation.

One year Lisa came with me to a national park Board meeting in Yosemite. Our friend John Huey, sustainability manager for Delaware North who lived in Modesto, drove his classic Jaguar up the mountain and took her around the park. She hiked solo down the Glacier Point Trail and said she was pleasantly struck by the atmosphere of camaraderie – people hiking up or down spoke and were very pleasant to each other.

Yosemite National Park is one of the most spectacular places in America. Reportedly when the first Europeans saw the Yosemite Valley, a panorama of beautiful meadows cradled between giant rock mountains rising a mile straight up into the air, with a river running through it, they became even more convinced that they were highly favored by God. They removed the local Native tribes, most prominently the Ahwahnee, and declared that such a gift sealed the covenant of Manifest Destiny, that God had given them the North American continent to subdue and occupy coast to coast. How nefariously we use God!

At the end of the conference, Delaware North hosted a book signing for me in the lobby of the Ahwahnee. The historic hotel is rich in wood and ambience, and one of my greatest pleasures came when one of the doormen welcomed us back on our second or third visit. It's a very good feeling to be recognized at the Ahwahnee. With rooms starting around $400, it's the kind of place we were able to enjoy largely because our hosts offered Board members complimentary lodging.

Afterwards Lisa and I drove down the mountain to San Francisco, where we planned to meet up with Dr. Finney who was teaching at UC Berkeley. We were all planning to visit the Rosie the Riveter World War II Homefront National Historical Park where we hoped to meet the second most famous park ranger in the world, Betty Reid Soskin. At age 95, Ranger Soskin was also the oldest park ranger still working.

She was among the first women to enter the workforce during WWII, when most of the men were already in the war and the women were called upon to help build planes and ships. Ranger Soskin had helped conceptualize and develop that park at the very place where the shipyards had been, and gave first-person accounts to visitors who came from all over the world to see her.

When we met it was a love fest, as she admired what Frank and I were accomplishing, bringing the contributions of African Americans in the parks to light. Dr. Finney and her friend the artist Marguerite Brown took Lisa and me to dinner at a seafood restaurant on San Francisco Bay, after which we said our goodbyes and Lisa flew home to Atlanta while I flew home to Fort Lauderdale.

A few years later, we invited Ranger Soskin to speak at a panel at the Congressional Black Caucus Annual Legislative Weekend in DC. She flew in the night before for our 10 a.m. session. When Frank and I arrived at the meeting room Ranger Soskin was already there, though the park superintendent who accompanied her on the trip told us they got in very late the night before. Her stamina rivals that of a motivated 20-year old, and the audience was in rapt attention to her story.

I moderated the panel which included: Director Bob Stanton; Dr. Finney, by then a member of the Congressionally chartered National Parks Advisory Board; Cassius Cash, Superintendent of Great Smoky Mountains National Park; Rachel Stewart, a leading young underwater explorer; and Clarence Fluker from the White House Council on Environmental Quality. Congressman Alcee Hastings fell in love with Ranger Soskin, as did everyone who met her.

President Obama invited Ranger Soskin to join him in lighting the National Christmas Tree at the White House in 2015. Ranger Soskin told us later that the image of her great-grandmother, Leontine, born into slavery in 1846, was uppermost in her mind that night. Her grandmother helped raise her and lived to see her married with children.

She touched the picture of her grandmother in her pocket when she met the President, bringing the Black story in America full circle in that moment – from an enslaved African to a President of the United States of African descent. Her two grand-daughters were in the audience, among millions witnessing this singular moment.

Ranger Soskin said that, when she and the President hugged, he held her hand and pressed something into her palm, gently closing her fingers over it. When she opened her hand, she looked down in wonder to find his Seal of the President of the United States.

Writing the story for my blog in the Huffington Post, I decided to do a little research about a rumor I'd heard that President Obama was also descended from an enslaved person, and sure enough, there it was on Ancestry.com.

The President's history has been traced back 14 generations ON HIS WHITE MOTHER'S SIDE to the first African enslaved for life in America, John Punch! I included that in the story which blew a lot of people's minds as they wrote and told me.

Ranger Soskin had to prove her strength and her wits once again when a burglar climbed up the wall of her apartment in the middle of the night and broke into her bedroom where she was sleeping. He attacked her and demanded the medal. Ranger Soskin fought him off, leapt out of bed and made it to her bathroom where she locked herself in.

Looking around for a weapon in case he was able to get in, all she saw was her iron. She quickly plugged it in, set it to the highest setting and stood waiting for the thief with her iron in her hand. Her plan was to sear him wherever she could. Thankfully, he did not get in, but he got her medal and left.

When the local community heard about the attack on our beloved Ranger they were outraged. We were all equally awed by her alacrity and quick thinking. President Obama promptly sent her another medal to replace the one stolen.

Once I was asked to speak at a conference where land managers were going to unveil a new program intended for "urban" people. I'm not sure when that word came into use, but in my experience it's usually referring to Black and Brown people. Iantha was also scheduled to speak there.

I usually try to arrive a day before I'm speaking so I can mingle with the people and get a feel for where their head is and what their priorities are. Iantha arrived before me and I walked into the conference room where a session was going on, to let her know I'd arrived.

When I sat down, I heard the older White gentleman on stage who was identified in the program as a demographer, beginning to describe the future populations that these land managers would be serving. Iantha and I were among a handful of Blacks in the room of about 200 people.

Steam began to build up and start coming out of my ears when I heard the gentleman saying, "They will mostly be immigrants. They will have lower education levels and lower economic worth. They will..." followed by a bunch more negatives.

I turned to look around the room and saw a pall of depression falling over the audience. I felt like leaping up and confronting him right there, but I restrained myself. I would have my turn and full control of the stage next day.

Next morning I began sweetly, recounting the things the presenter had said. Then I stated,

"I am the immigrant he described. I came from Jamaica with little more than a high school education, a single mother with a seven-year-old daughter and $1 in my pocketbook. And NO ONE WOULD ARGUE that I have done as much, if not more, for the public lands system than ANYONE in this room."

I told them how, through multiple television and radio appearances, innumerable articles we've written, interviews we've given, advocacy work we've done, books we've written and tours we've organized that introduced people to the parks, we've reached millions of people, many of whom say they'd never even heard about the national parks until we showed up.

"Many Black people told us that, before we came along, it never even occurred to them that they could go to the Grand Canyon or any of the places you're protecting," I said, with sarcastic emphasis on the last word. "So there's more than one way of looking at the numbers and the coming demographic shift."

A professor who'd been doing research on the agency's workforce reported that the employees said flatly that they were not interested in doing the outreach that the project needed to succeed. Yet everyone proceeded just as if that wasn't relevant and I was forced to point it out.

Oh the games people play. When Frank and I fell into the environmental field, I assumed that it would be free of race prejudice, since we're talking about the most fundamental commonality of life. I cannot begin to describe my shock and dismay to find out how thoroughly entrenched it is in this sector as well.

I've been in boardrooms where the top executive presented exhaustively about the future of national parks and how their wellbeing depended on the extent to which Black and Hispanic Americans embrace them. Then he concluded, "Sadly, they are not."

"What have you done to engage people over all the years I've been telling you that is what is needed?" I demanded.

Sometimes I feel that Black and Brown Americans are better off than many of our wealthier White counterparts, because I simply cannot imagine the mental gymnastics they have to go through to square away their prejudiced and destructive actions against their fellow citizens. And many are perfectly nice, wonderful upstanding people who would be insulted if you show them how prejudiced they are. I'm glad I don't have to bear that burden.

In 2019, a young Black woman and a young Hispanic woman working in conservation organizations called me within two weeks of each other and asked, "What should I tell my leadership about why we need diversity training and to be more inclusive?"

I responded, "Tell them I said we use the word 'leader' much too liberally. A real leader looks ahead, sees the challenges and makes strategic plans to head them off. With the majority of members of White environmental organizations averaging 68 years old, they're presiding over the death of their organizations. If at this late date they're still asking those questions, they're no leaders at all."

Once an organization brought me out to Boston to help develop the strategy for their diversity efforts. They were distressed that their attempts had not succeeded. I asked them to describe some of their efforts so far and they said, "Well, for example, we needed to hire an accountant in New York City. We're trying to be more inclusive, yet we still wound up with a White person in the position."

How could that be, I asked, when New York City, the financial capital of the world, is teeming with financial professionals of every race?

"Well," the lead person responded sheepishly, "The manager that they were going to work with wanted someone he'd feel comfortable with."

Of course! If the people who're already in are all White and want people who are just like them that they'll be comfortable with, that's not a recipe for progress.

****

CHAPTER TWENTY-TWO

When Eco-Diversity Magazine announced me as one of the 2018 Top African Americans in Conservation and Environmental Justice, they cited my "unapologetic voice for the inclusion of Americans of color in conservation." I sometimes found myself feeling downright disagreeable. Many times after Frank and I had just given a spirited presentation about how eagerly African Americans respond to the invitation to the outdoors, one of the first questions we'd get from the floor was,

"What do we need to do to get minorities involved?" That was usually followed by a story about how difficult it was to interest 'minorities' in the outdoors.

Depending on the level of engagement I was feeling in the room I might ask,

"What have you done so far?"

Invariably the answer was, "Well, we talked. . ." and the story would reveal that a group of White people had talked to each other about how they needed to reach out to communities of color. And that would be it. They would be completely convinced that they'd really tried and it was just too bad that more of "those people" weren't interested.

At other times if I was just too chagrined I might blurt, "Excuse me. I just spent an hour up here telling you..."

Over the years some of our White friends confided that they really respected how we just kept going because they wouldn't have been able to take it. But we were trying to accomplish something. The job wasn't done and it would only become more urgent, the longer we ignored the signs of change all around us.

As the temperature heated up, we began to notice an increase in the number of squirrels in South Florida, where I didn't even remember seeing squirrels when we moved there in 1985. We began seeing the occasional iguana, and in a few years they've overrun the place and become such a nuisance that counties are encouraging homeowners to slaughter them. Since they are often as long as four feet with powerful claws and tail, killing them is fraught with danger, and no instructions have been given for how one might dispose of them, once killed.

When we first drove up to the Great Smoky Mountains National Park in the 1990s we marveled at the thick forests of tall hemlock trees across the ridge. When we drove the same route a few years later after the rising temperatures had allowed a beetle called the wooly adelgid to thrive, the forest was a shadow of itself, with many of the trees stark white, dead or dying.

When we went to Glacier National Park in Montana a few years after our first time, it was horrifying to see how the glaciers had retreated. There was almost no snow cover where before there had been ice packed on the mountain peaks.

Maybe because people are spending so much time indoors – from the house to the car to the office to the car back home – we are not as aware of the changes as we might otherwise be. I often think how our ancestors, and even our recent forbears, spent the majority of their time outdoors, how they studied the night sky and determined how the movement of the planets and stars were directly tied to events on Earth. As Dr. Musgrave warned, we're taking most of our information from "content" created by other fallible human beings, drilling farther and farther down into minutiae while missing the magnificent spectacle of which we are part.

I was driving home from the airport one night and decided to take a new route. Passing by The Science of Mind church, I saw the topic of the sermon for the coming Sunday, which so intrigued me that I decided I was going to be there for that. The service had already started when I got there, and as I walked in I heard the minister in the pulpit say,

"I don't know why people think it is only that part of their communication that begins with, 'Dear God' that God hears. God is reading your mind and hearing your thoughts at all times."

It was a light bulb moment. From then on, I tried to really tune in and see what my thoughts were, and change them if they were negative. Not long afterwards I read Eckhart Tolle's book, "The Power of Now," in which he pointed out that the mind was intended to be our tool, but has now become our master.

He said we're always looking ahead to the future with anticipation or dread, or looking back in the past with nostalgia or regret. In so doing, we miss the power of the present moment in which we are alive and creating what comes next. I found that so powerful that I've worked at practicing it ever since.

While working on the project to restore the Everglades, we were invited by Mike Davis, Deputy Assistant Secretary of the Army for Civil Works, to meet with him at the Pentagon. Frank was busy so our friend Anne Humphrey, who was working as our administrative assistant, came with me. It was one of the few times we had help. Anne was very glamorous and high fashion and after she first came to Everglades National Park with us she said, "I thought the Everglades was swamp and snakes and grunge, only to find that it's beauty and history and wonder."

Exactly. You don't know what you don't know.

When I mentioned to her that we might have a chance to meet with the Secretary of the Interior, she asked innocently, "Is she a good decorator?"

That makes perfect sense, as it's the context in which people generally hear "interior" used. I explained to her that the interior meant inside the country and, in particular, referred to more than 630 million acres of land protected in the National Park System and wildlife refuges, and managed by the Bureau of Land Management and the U.S. Army Corps of Engineers. The forests are managed by the United States Department of Agriculture, a separate agency.

It's symptomatic of the mystique built up around the outdoors that an "interpreter" or "interpretation" refers not to the translator of a foreign language, but to a person who tells the story of the natural and cultural history of a place.

We went to the Department of Interior and met with former director Bob Stanton, a passionate advocate for national parks as the "open university system" of America. Director Stanton had been working on diversity since the 60s when, as a freshman ranger, he was tapped by the revered Interior Secretary Stewart Udall, for whom the building is named, to begin the integration of the parks.

Young Mr. Stanton was dispatched to The Grand Teton National Park in Jackson, Wyoming, which even now is one of the Whitest places in the country. He acquitted himself extraordinarily well and rose through the ranks to become Director under President Clinton. Whatever we asked of him, Director Stanton was willing to do and he stood as a complete contradiction to the fallacy that Americans of color do not care about the outdoors or wilderness.

Near the turn of the 21st Century Iantha hosted a conference at the Algonquin Training Center, a beautiful secluded place on the Potomac. It was awesome and, when some of the young people from Los Angeles came and saw the surroundings, they were awestruck.

"In our neighborhood when you talk about a park, it's a little piece of hard scrabble ground with a few spindly trees and it's dangerous, because that's where the drug addicts hang out," said one young man.

The young people were astonished that someone of the Director's stature was interested in them and cared that they should be exposed to nature and beauty as potential future caretakers of our national parks. Comparing their formative experiences with my own, I wonder how equipped they will be to deal with the crisis we are creating for them.

Next we went to the Pentagon to discuss with Mr. Davis the restoration of the Everglades and the necessary involvement of Americans of color. The rigidity that we saw there, in the structure of the building and the severity of dress and attitudes, seemed like the antithesis of anything natural. I value the work that people in the Pentagon do, but I won't mind if I never have to go there again.

The National Park Service was preparing to celebrate its 100th Anniversary on August 25, 2016, with a lot of fanfare. The agency planned to launch a big campaign called "Find Your Park," to engage the public, mostly on social media. We let the leadership know through face to face meetings, by raising it at advocacy Board meetings and liberally writing about it, that such a campaign would miss large numbers of people, especially those who most needed the information. How are you going to "find" something you don't know about and are not looking for?

Frank and I know hundreds of environmental leaders of color across the country who are working magic in their communities with very little exposure, funding or support. I was inspired to create an entity that would connect us all and make us easier to find. So I called up 50 of our closest friends and invited them to join us in forming the Diverse Environmental Leaders Speakers Bureau. Forty-nine said yes, and the one person who declined already had a different plan.

As they were from all over the country, we needed to get everyone together and spend some time bonding. The most bondable place I can think of in the world is Grand Canyon National Park, so we negotiated with the Park Service to provide diversity and inclusion training for their staff. In return they offered us lodging at the Albright Training Center, a collection of apartments and cottages laid out in a forest of pine trees. The agency was supportive of the Bureau, which brought a high level of expertise together in one place.

We raised $90,000 to launch the Bureau, approximately the same amount we'd raised to put on the Breaking the Color Barrier Conference. Most of it came from my colleagues on Boards I served on, nonprofit organizations and corporations that were our allies. It helped provide transportation for 35 speakers and our support team including Event Planner Damita Holbrook, who took care of all the details so that Frank and I could be free to handle what we needed to. Damita was our event planner since our first Keeping It Wild Gala in Atlanta, and she and her team were highly proficient.

The majority of the speakers were visiting the Grand Canyon for the first time, and excitement was high. Those who'd been part of Breaking the Color Barrier were excited to see each other again, and everyone else was eager to be part of the dynamic group.

There were seasoned veterans, such as Majora Carter, and young people just starting out, such as Miss Teen Navajo Nation Krishel Augustine who lived at Grand Canyon. She'd just graduated high school and already produced a Junior Ranger CD that was sold in parks across the country. She wrote and produced her own songs and accompanied herself on instruments.

Krishel's aunt Rena Bob offered to make us a Native dinner and came over with her sisters bearing trays of fry bread, pots of spicy ground meats and all the trimmings. We felt so honored.

For four days we toured the park and held training sessions during which all the speakers presented their area of specialty. Park Service staff included the Assistant Director of Workforce,

Relevancy and Inclusion, Rose Pruitt, and the Superintendent of Little Rock Central High School National Historic Site, Robin White, who marveled at the experts we'd brought together.

To top it all off, park concessionaire Xanterra, which operates the lodging and amenities in the park, threw a reception for us in the Kiva Room of the Thunderbird Lodge. If there is anything better than being warmly embraced with wine and hors d'oeuvres flowing, it's being able to take a few steps to the door in your finery and high heels and see the Grand Canyon laid out before you. Wow!!

We launched the Speakers Bureau at the National Press Club on August 25, 2014, exactly two years to the day from the Centennial. We were joined by supporters from the Park Service, the Forest Service and multiple environmental organizations.

Speakers came from the four corners of the country. Irela Bague, an expert on water and climate issues, came from Miami; Stephen Shobe, a mountaineer who has reached the summit of the highest mountains on four continents, came from Northern California; Jarid Manos, author and founder of Restoration Not Incarceration, came from Fort Worth, Texas; Captain Bill Pinkney came from Puerto Rico; and tourism professional Loan Sewer came from St. Thomas, U.S. Virgin Islands. Our special invited guest Ranger Shelton Johnson came down from his mountain aerie in Yosemite National Park.

Speaking from the podium I told our audience that, if they took advantage of the talents of the Bureau and engaged us to train and sensitize their staff to the nuances of outreach in non-White communities, we could arrive at the Centennial date two years later in an entirely different country. I emphasized that one of the most consistent explanations we'd heard for why more people of color don't engage with the outdoors or environment is that they don't see people like themselves in stories about environmentalists, and don't feel welcome in that space.

"We can help make sure that people know they're invited, that they have a legacy to enjoy and protect in these sacred places," I said.

After the launch, speakers went up to Capitol Hill to meet with their Members of Congress and engage them with how much we care about the environment, and how concerned we are that so many in our communities are neither knowledgeable about what is coming, nor involved in efforts to deal with it. We suggested ways they could help make sure that changed.

The speakers toured DC and visited multiple national parks including: the White House (yes, it's in a national park!); Ford Theater where President Lincoln was shot by John Wilkes Booth; and the Petersen House across the street, where he died the next day.

Just as I had with Pickup & GO! I sat back and waited for the calls to roll in to book speakers. Once again, NOT! We got a few engagements, but nothing of the magnitude we envisioned, or the amount that would build the needed momentum.

****

CHAPTER TWENTY-THREE

In 2015 we got a call from Nick Aumen, one of our colleagues working on Everglades restoration, letting us know that President Obama was coming to the park, and inviting us to come down! Wow!! I am all about the egalitarianism of the parks, but that day I confess I didn't mind that the park was closed to the general public, and only about 100 people were invited.

One of our top five favorite park ranger friends, Alan Scott, is the Chief of Resource Education and Interpretation at Everglades, and he generally leads official tours of the park. We waited for the president in an area near the Visitor Center overlooking a wide swath of sawgrass that we'd seen many times before. But that day it was vivified by the President, whose lanky, relaxed figure and kind handsome face transfixed me. I was fortunate enough to be sitting right in front of him two rows back and I know my face was radiating joy the entire time.

He talked about the urgency of addressing the climate crisis and described the measures his administration was taking to reduce pollution by investing in clean energy technologies. He announced that he was adding the home of Marjory Stoneman Douglas, the heroine of the Everglades who woke up the nation to its peril, to the Park System as a National Historic Site. Yaay.

The President's security detail included a Secret Service agent that was the widest human being Frank or I had ever seen. We laughed that we definitely did not want to run afoul of him.

When President Obama came down the barricade shaking hands, I made sure I was right in front this time. I told the Secret Service agent ahead of him that I really had to get a picture with him.

"So give your phone to someone behind you and ask them to take it," he said.

Well, duh!

I turned around and saw a beautiful young lady behind me, handed her my phone and asked her to please get my picture with the President. As he approached I searched frantically in my mind for something meaningful I might say to him in the few seconds I'd have. I got it when he was just a few steps away.

When he shook my hand, I said, "Thank you, Mr. President, for creating the Pullman National Monument."

Pullman protects one of the first planned industrial cities in his hometown Chicago, and he'd used his executive authority to declare it part of the National Park System just a few months earlier. As a member of the Board of Trustees of the National Parks Conservation Association I'd helped work to get that done.

He chuckled, and went on to shake Frank's hand, saying, "Good day. How are you, sir?" He was so deferential and respectful.

And then I had a mishap which I have to chalk up to fate, because my phone malfunctioned just as I was trying to take the picture of the President shaking Frank's hand. I know I would have gone ballistic if I hadn't got my picture, but Frank was so cool.

"I had the experience," he said. "I just know Dad would be so proud."

Our friends who got to shake the President's hand included Rangers Sabrina Diaz, Linda Friar and Paula Nelson Shokar. We were so excited that we said we were never going to wash our hands ever again. That lasted about 30 minutes.

I wonder what the group of Fifth Graders who were on the Anhinga Trail did after they got to high five the President.

What a great day!

Early 2016 we got a call from a friend who said that for so many years she had heard Iantha and me talk about all the environmental work going on in communities of color which needed to be elevated to national attention. Now she was in a position to help. She proposed to bring together a group of environmental, civil rights and social justice leaders among others, focused on getting Presidential action.

She wanted to know if we'd be interested in serving as the hosts and if she could send out the invitation under our signature, along with a group of co-hosts including Rue Mapp and Juan Martinez, a rising leader who'd recently been named a National Geographic Young Explorer. Of course our answer was a resounding YES!

The Obama administration was proactive about getting more young people and minorities involved with the outdoors and environment, and one of our friends, Julie Williams, headed up the Department of Interior's "Every Kid in a Park" program that gave passes to fourth graders so that they and their families could visit the parks.

In March 2016, we met in Washington, DC and launched the Next100 Coalition. In its first century the National Park Service had done an excellent job of protecting land and historical places, and now the challenge was to make those places known and embraced by the entire country. We developed the criteria we'd like to see in place and asked President Obama to sign a Presidential Memorandum to make it official.

We held meetings with Members of Congress and worked closely with the White House Council on Environmental Quality headed by Ms. Christy Goldfuss. Meanwhile we coordinated events in our communities around the country to raise awareness about the issues.

Early January 2017 we got the good news: the Presidential Memorandum Promoting Diversity and Inclusion in Our National Parks, National Forests, and Other Public Lands and Waters was issued January 12, 2017. It laid out precise guidance to the managers of the public lands system and gave them a mandate to focus on including more historical sites that tell the contributions of Americans of color, and to make sure that all their programs are inclusive of diverse populations.

The Coalition included Dr. Finney, and one of the happiest days of my life was the day we got an e-mail from Ms. Goldfuss' office, saying she wanted to set up a time to call and thank us for our leadership and discuss our vision going forward. Dr. Finney got a similar request.

Wow!! We could stick a pin right there. I felt that the mission Frank and I set for ourselves back in 1995 was very close to being accomplished when the White House was recognizing our efforts. Coalition members gathered in DC later to celebrate with Manager Goldfuss and her team, members of Congress, and representatives of major environmental organizations.

In January 2017, I attended an environmental conference in Miami where I'd been invited to speak. Frank and I had been going every year since 1997 and had worked very hard to sensitize the planners to include the Black and Hispanic populations which comprise a substantial part of the makeup of South Florida. Things had seemed quite promising before we moved to Atlanta, and the group comprising more than 40 of the nation's top environmental groups had presented Frank and me with the George Barley Award for leadership. Mr. Barley and his wife Mary were committed to the restoration of the Everglades, but he'd died tragically in a plane crash. Years later, Mary Barley would be the first person to say

"Yes" when I asked for help to launch the Speakers Bureau, providing us with seed money of $2500.

I hadn't been to the conference in maybe 10 years and, to my amazement, when I walked in I saw literally the same White people from a decade earlier, with a sprinkling of even fewer Black people, none of whom was in a leadership position. On top of that they were talking about the very same things, as if the climate and the outlook had not changed dramatically in the intervening time.

When it was my turn I could hardly control my outrage. I recounted what I'd learned about New Orleans – how the authorities knew before Katrina hit that the levies wouldn't stand up to a Category Five storm, and ordered thousands of body bags without telling the people how serious the threat was. I said that in a few years that could be Miami or Fort Lauderdale buying thousands of body bags.

Then the mayor of Homestead City, located between the Atlantic and Everglades National Park, who was also on the panel stated,

"Elected officials only respond when people are reaching out to them, knocking on their doors, letting them know they care about an issue. If people care about this, they need to be reaching out to their representatives and letting them know."

Well, blow me down. I thought it was the other way around – that the government with all its resources and our tax dollars would gather information and use it to make the wisest decisions for the people. So now I started breaking it down in my writing and asked people, "If you had a chance to do something BEFORE Katrina that would reduce the loss of life and property, would you have done it?"

I shared the vast array of knowledge we had accumulated and the politician's own words and encouraged people to organize and petition their local and national governments to take action before it was too late.

I was serving on many prestigious national Boards which don't pay Board members, though I insisted that they pay for my travel and lodging. I figured it was a good trade-off because having a seat at the table meant that I could have an influence on things that were important to me, such as protection of the national parks, inclusion of all people in the benefits, and sounding the alarm about the degradation of our environment.

Once my Mom asked me, "Why do you care so much if Americans don't know what they have?"

I thought about it and didn't have a good answer, except that I cared passionately. Those principles of equality and fairness that I absorbed growing up in Jamaica, the benefits I had derived from nature that were amplified by seeing the national parks – all of those things counted. In the years since we "discovered" the parks in 1995, we had traveled to more than 185 of them from Florida to Alaska and the U.S. Virgin Islands, and learned that the entire history of the development of America is in the parks and historic sites.

For example, every Jamaican knows Bob Marley's "Buffalo Soldiers" lyrics, but few people even in America know that the Buffalo Soldiers were real; that they were Black; and that they were largely responsible for fighting the Native Americans and protecting the White people migrating to the West. This knowledge dramatically undercuts the popular story of the brave White man riding west and taking his wife and children and a few slaves with him.

We found the Buffalo Soldiers story told in parks, including Fort Davis National Historic Site in Texas where they lived and worked. I burst into tears when I looked out at the same view of upthrust rocks known as hoodoos that the Buffalo Soldiers looked at when they were there. I wondered what their thoughts were and said a prayer of thanksgiving to their souls.

We found them in Alaska at Klondike Gold Rush National Historical Park in Alaska where they were sent to keep the peace in The Klondike Gold Rush in the late 19th century, and we found them again in the Sierra Nevada Mountains of California where they were sent to protect the first national parks in 1903. Visiting the Giant Sequoia forests in Sequoia National Park high up in the mountains, walking among those sacred groves of trees, some of which are more than 2,000 years old and were alive at the time that Jesus walked on Earth, is a mind-blowing experience.

When we learned that the Buffalo Soldiers, under orders of the U.S. Army, saved these trees from being cut down by lumbermen and ranchers, my heart swelled with pride. I can only imagine the interactions that went on between rich White men and these Black soldiers in such incredibly remote locations. But they triumphed, and now every year millions of people from all over the world travel up the mountain to the park to revel in the forests that they saved.

We brought this, and scores of other stories about the contributions that Black, Hispanic and Asian Americans made to the development of America, into public view at a time when very few people were talking about them. We also helped turn the tide in people calling our ancestors slaves, pointing out that nobody is born a slave as everyone is born a child of God with the Light of God within them. We said that to call our ancestors slaves was to continue to disrespect them and deny their humanity. Instead we wanted the onus to be placed on the people who enslaved them, and after years of making this argument it became very satisfying to be in meetings and hear people refer to "the enslaved people" instead.

The Boards and exposure gave us the platform to help make these changes.

When Mom found out I was going to all these meetings and not getting paid she was apoplectic.

"You mean you're leaving your house for three, four days at a time and coming back with no money?"

Luckily she didn't say she must have raised some sort of an idiot which, if looked at a certain way, had some merit. Truth is, we were striving to follow our heart and do what was needed and make a living from it. On balance it worked out, because our service enabled us to have close to a 360-degree understanding of the problem and to present that in our speeches and workshops.

The pressure from being able to see the environmental changes and know that worse was coming, while being unable to rouse the masses or politicians to act, could have taken a toll on us, but fortunately we had the very place where this all began to save us - nature. We went out for our walk most early mornings, many times by the New River and sometimes into the neighboring community of Sailboat Bend, the oldest community in Fort Lauderdale. There was a memorial in our marina commemorating the spot where the city started, after Native Americans killed the first colonizers.

The neighborhood had retained many of its old Live Oak trees, with huge branches growing parallel to the ground, and Resurrection ferns that looked like dead leaves on the trunk, but burst into brilliant life when it rained.

I was somewhat more hotheaded and spontaneous than Frank, who could always be counted on to be more balanced. He was never impressed by the accolades people bestowed on us because he said the same people who love you today can call you the worst person in the world tomorrow.

Another of the best things about Frank was how he allowed me to be free. He'd told me early on, "I came into your life to expand it, not to restrict it." When we got married I did not want a wedding ring because I tend to lose jewelry and other things easily, and he did not insist. If someone made a pass at me I could tell him and he'd laugh and say,

"Well, if I was the only one that noticed you we'd be in bad shape."

I couldn't help it – I would involuntarily start out every presentation with a tribute to Frank and say how much I love and appreciate him. I noticed that audiences really loved that, maybe because there is so much cynicism about marriage that they enjoyed seeing a happy mature couple.

****

CHAPTER TWENTY-FOUR

In March 2018 we were scheduled to speak at the conference of a coalition of environmental organizations, Everyone's Environment, at the University of North Carolina, Asheville. They proposed to take us on tour of the Carl Sandburg Home National Historic Site before our presentation. A few weeks before the scheduled time, I received an email from a woman who identified herself as Tanya Cummings saying,

"I cannot tell you how excited I am that you are coming to our area.... Like you, I have an affinity for nature, and relocated to the greater Asheville area from Los Angeles (and beyond) because of the national parks. The Carl Sandburg Home is in my backyard.... I'm looking forward to joining you on your adventure to the Home as well as to hear you speak at UNC!"

What a great welcome!

When we arrived at the Home with our hostess Deborah Miles from UNC, we were greeted by Tanya and her friends Flo Mayberry and Kathy Avery. We joined with other visitors to tour the gracious white house on a hill overlooking a very salubrious valley, including a pond in which ducks swam.

I'd done my research and knew the site was carved out of the hills by enslaved Africans on behalf of Christopher Memminger, the

Secretary of the Confederacy, in the 1830s. I chuckled at the storyline that Memminger "brought" his "slaves" with him from Charleston, considering how my ancestors would have done all the backbreaking bringing and building.

The story was that Sandburg's wife bought the house and got everything set up before he even saw it, then she invited him to come home where he could continue his writing and advocacy. He was a champion for civil and human rights, advocated equality and a living wage for Black Americans and campaigned tirelessly to end child labor. Until then I had completely blocked out of my mind that 80 years ago children were a big part of the labor force, spending their days toiling in factories in industrializing countries.

Taking in the view from the house sloping down to the tranquil pond, I couldn't help thinking what it must have cost the enslaved people in effort, maybe even life and limb, to build. So as the tour progressed and the park ranger talked about the Sandburg family and even their prized herd of goats, I waited to hear more about the Black laborers.

We toured the "slave quarters" and the wash house and I noticed that all of us Black women gathered around the old washtubs, as if to honor our foremothers and the countless hours of labor they must have expended there.

When I realized that they were barely going to get a mention in the story, I asked the ranger to tell us more about them. She said they knew very little about the Black people. I told her that was not good enough, that the park needed to present the full story. Imagine honoring a man so far ahead of his time, a crusader for equality, and dishonoring what he stood for by leaving out central characters based on "race" and position.

I strive not to be offensive, though I'm uncompromising in making my point. The ranger said there was actually a community of descendants not too far away. Well, there you go, I said, start there. I suggested that the park needed to devote some resources to connect with that community and help them unearth and share their story. Later Tanya told me that when she heard me speak so confidently and directly she thought, "I have got to get to know this woman."

That night as we spoke at the university, I noticed her and Flo in the audience. She was leaning forward, eyes glowing, taking in everything Frank and I were saying. When we opened it up for questions, she introduced herself and said she was so inspired by the experiences we shared and the need to engage the whole country in the enjoyment and protection of the public lands that she wanted to help.

At the reception that followed, I saw her and her friends sitting at a table that included a young White man from a conservation organization who'd been with us at the Sandburg Home. Just then one of our old friends from Atlanta, George Briggs, Executive Director of the North Carolina Arboretum, came over to talk with us, and said he was very interested in engaging with more Black people in the area.

I took him by the hand and led him over to the table where Tanya was sitting and said, "Here are the people you're looking for. Talk with them."

One of the great things about being in the environmental field for so long is that wherever we go we have friends who'll make the effort to come and see us. Our friend Julie Mayfield from Atlanta who'd moved to Asheville with her husband Jim and won a seat on the Asheville City Council was also in the audience and we had a grand reunion. We left Asheville on a wave of love and drove to Charlotte to spend some time with my god sister Monica who'd recently retired from a career as a banker.

Not long after, Tanya called and told me that she and her fiancé Larry Pender decided to form an organization dedicated to helping people of color in Asheville get out and enjoy the voluptuous amount of nature in their own backyard. She said that when she talked to people in the area, they were reluctant to venture out because it wasn't something they'd done before. Considering that Asheville is the gateway to the Blue Ridge Mountains and the Great

Smoky Mountains, Tanya and Pender were determined to help change that.

In short order, they worked with others to create an organization called "Pathways to Parks," and expressly stated in the mission that their goal was to "carry on the mission of Frank and Audrey Peterman." Within a year they had grown so much and been so successful that they invited us to come back to a big community celebration, "It's Your Backyard: On the Doorstep of Paradise," on April 6, 2019.

Tanya and Pender suggested we come up a few days early and spend time with them at their home, which they've appropriately named "Paradise." Tucked into the hillside at the beginning of a dirt road, their splendid three-story wood home is reached by crossing a gurgling brook, overlooking a pond, surrounded by acres of rhododendron and azalea trees. Such luxury! Frank and I had our own flat downstairs and an elevator up to the third floor, and best of all I could sit on our balcony and listen to the stream which sounded just like my gully. Oh joy.

They took us to dinner at the historical Grove Park Inn where President Obama and First Lady Michelle had recently stayed. When we ordered and the server heard my accent, he told me that the cook was Jamaican and had just returned from vacation. Then he went and brought him out to meet us and we had a grand reunion, though we had never met before. Having Jamaica in common breaks down all barriers. Besides, I tend not to have many barriers anyway.

When we got to the event Saturday morning organized by Pathways to Parks and their collaborators at the Southern Appalachian Highlands Conservancy, we met a young man that we'd been hearing a lot of buzz about. Daniel White calls himself "The Blackalachian" after hiking the entire 2,189-mile Appalachian Trail from Georgia to Maine, with zero previous experience. With his dreadlocks and gold teeth, he was the exact opposite of the image of an American hiker, and had gone on to bike the 2,000 mile Underground Railroad Trail from Alabama to Canada, and visited the home of the Railroad's most famous "conductor," Harriet Tubman, in upstate New York.

He began his presentation by mentioning that there were "Living Legends" in the room, referring to me and Frank. What a great feeling. Combined with the fact that Outdoor Afro - which promotes healthful activities for African Americans in the outdoors - gave us their Lifetime Achievement Award in 2016, and that our grandson Yero is a rising conservationist with Greening Youth Foundation and was featured on the cover of Outdoor Retailer Magazine in the spring of 2019, it sure felt like we were getting closer to – mission accomplished!

We'd put our sailing dreams on hold for six years to be there for Mom, and Frank was with me every step of the way. Not once did he complain or say "I wish it was different." If I was traveling and Mom had a problem with her doctor or her medication or anything, she'd call him and he'd get right on it. Once I was speaking at the Grand Canyon for Black History Month and something came up that I'd usually address, and Frank stepped in and took care of it without missing a beat. I am so glad that we were able to be there for my mother.

One of the best and most poignant days of my life was the day she said to me, "You really stood up for me, Audrey. Thank you."

After a serious operation Mom had to go into a nursing home. Fortunately, it was just across the street from the assisted living facility where she'd lived for several years, so many of her friends and members of the staff could easily go over and see her. A young Jamaican woman named Helecia Charlton was like a daughter to her, and her stepmom Jean was Mom's strong right arm.

Early April 2017 I had a speaking engagement in New Orleans, and the weekend before we left Lisa and Yero flew down from Atlanta and Frank and I drove up from Fort Lauderdale to visit Mom. Yero wheeled her outside so she could feel the sun and we cheerfully talked about her life and how much she had done for us.

I'd always made sure to impress upon Lisa that the life we enjoy is a result of Mom having the strength and the bravery to leave the security of New Roads and take on the world. She paved the way for us and we regaled her with memories of all the fun times we had together.

When I left her that day I had the feeling I might never see her again. I did not regret the fact that she might die, as she was outspoken about being ready to go. She had suffered excruciating pain for many years and had only gotten worse. She was a woman of strong faith and a member of First Baptist Church in Poinciana for more than 20 years. She served in the Vivian Edge organization where she was elected president in 1999 and was a member of the Thursday Prayer Group.

Though health problems prevented her from physically attending church services, Mom remained confident in the church and her relationships. Many people she met at her home and in treatment took special interest in her because of their mutual connection to First Baptist. Friends and officials from the church visited her and prayed with her constantly. Some of her closest friends were her church brethren, chief among them Angela Watson who was like a sister to her. Frank and I were a three-hour drive away but Mom always knew that, if she needed someone, Ms. Angela and her husband Charles would be there for her. So would Ms. Elaine Tyrell and her husband George, among others.

We were in New Orleans three days and talked with Mom every chance we got. We expressed our love and gratitude for each other. That morning, while we were at the airport getting ready to go home, I got an urgent call from the nursing home that she was going, and that if we wanted to see her we needed to get there right away. By the time we boarded the plane, they called and said she was gone.

My heart was full to bursting. I was so grateful that her soul had escaped the confines of her physical body. No more pain and suffering for my Mom. She had dreamed of being with God and actively visualized her life in Heaven. Her friend Ruth had died very suddenly the year before and Mom never got over it. Now I envisioned them being together again with Mama and Mass D and all the friends who'd gone before. Thank God Frank was with me.

I counted it all success when Lisa said to me later, "Mom, you set the bar high, caring for Granny."

Mom had made her funeral arrangements and paid for them years before. All we had to do was take care of her homegoing celebrations. Her brother, my Uncle Ricky Butler, who is much younger than me and has made a great success of himself in New York, was very supportive of his sister and helped make everything easier financially. Mom and Lisa had always been close and through the years of her illness when Lisa visited her she'd climb into bed with her, and I think that was the greatest comfort of all.

It wasn't until after she died that I knew how much Mom had suffered as an immigrant, and how much she loved me. Because I didn't grow up with her my first allegiance was to my grandmother, Mama, and I imagine she had some feelings of regret about that. But I understood that she couldn't take me with her. I was much better off growing up in Rose Hill with Mama who was much more mellow, than growing up with Mom in Kingston while she was striving to make a living.

Going through Mom's things I found a pamphlet from Grace Conservative Baptist Church in Nanuet that carried a feature story about her. It talked about how she'd arrived in New York with very high anticipation, but when she got to the airport the friend that she expected to stay with was not there to meet her. She had no way of knowing what had happened.

I pictured my poor Mom sitting in JFK airport all alone and bewildered in a sea of strange faces, sights and sounds. She sat there for hours until finally her friend's daughter showed up and told her that her mother had suffered a nervous breakdown. She took her to their house in Harlem and Mom said when she woke up next morning and looked outside she started to cry and was ready to go back home right away. She had never before seen that much concrete and no greenery.

She said that for months all she wanted to do was go back home, but she didn't have any prospects to go back to. She was working as a domestic to send money home to Mama and me while taking care of her own needs, paying her friend rent and paying a lawyer to get her immigration papers.

Mom had come to America on a six-week visitor's visa and overstayed her time at great risk. She said she felt extremely vulnerable at all times because anyone who knew her immigration status could manipulate her with the threat of reporting her to the Immigration and Naturalization Service. Still she persisted and survived, and I am eternally grateful to her.

It took me 14 months after Mom died to realize that she was gone, and we didn't need to stick around anymore to help her. I was actually taking a shower when it burst into my mind, "Wait a minute, we can go now!" For all that time my mind was on pause, still expecting to hear her call, still wondering if she had what she needed and if she might need my help.

"We can go now!" I came out of the shower yelling to Frank.

"What?"

"We can go now! Mom is gone!"

He looked at me a little strangely but said, "OK. Where do you want to go?'

Well suddenly that was a loaded question. I realized I no longer had the same passion for going sailing, plus I realized that sailing is a lot of work, and so is taking care of a boat. What I really wanted to do was go back to Jamaica and spend time immersed in the peace and tranquility of my roots.

I must confess that there was a time when I was so consumed with what I was doing in America that I almost forgot my homeland. I have Rhema to thank for this next phase of our lives. She came to visit many times in New York, Atlanta, and Fort Lauderdale and would always ask, "When are you coming home?"

At some point the question felt a little jarring because I didn't really feel I had that much to go home to. I had Auntie B and her children but I didn't know them very well, and besides them there were no pressing connections.

Then Rhema's daughter Jonelle, a Sergeant in the Marine Corps, got married in Jamaica in 2009 so of course I had to go home for that. So did Audrey and Cammal. Our friend Grandlin and her beautiful daughter Debi-Ann Newell who was studying medicine in Cuba were also there. It was a grand reunion.

We were all staying at Rhema and Tom's house, walking down memory lane and enjoying the closeness. Rhema is an avid gardener and every inch of ground at her place is occupied by the most gorgeous flowers or a fruit, vegetable or spice tree. I literally stood in her kitchen doorway and reached out and picked a breadfruit. Tom kept us liberally supplied with coconut water and we ate and drank to our hearts' content.

The one thing that was hard for me is that they don't have hot showers. When I mentioned this Rhema said, "Well, Sheena has flats that she rents that have hot water."

Wait, what?

****

CHAPTER TWENTY-FIVE

Once again a few fateful words changed the trajectory of my life. We went immediately to visit Sheena and drove into a wonderland the likes of which I'd only seen at Hope Gardens in Kingston. From the moment her high white electric gates parted, I was agog. The long driveway was lined with a riotous array of bougainvillea in red, white, purple and orange, interspersed with large yellow buttercups. From either side of the driveway the land stretched away and I could see Julie mango, ackee, cashew, guinep and Otaheite apple trees and a variety of plums, guava and star fruit. Later I discovered soursop, sweetsop and five other varieties of mangoes.

The centerpiece of the garden was a huge guinep tree, with intertwined branches that covered 360 degrees. Blooming underneath were more bougainvilleas, orchids, impatiens and others I couldn't identify. Birds called from everywhere and perched in the guinep tree. I spotted a dozen hummingbirds and a Doctor Bird with long tail feathers that lives only in Jamaica, and an inquisitive banana quit came to visit. The ambience was of complete serenity and tranquility, a Garden of Eden hidden away from the rest of the world. Wow!! Before Iantha I might have said I felt like I'd died and gone to Heaven. Now I said "I'm in Heaven and I didn't even have to die!"

Since I'd last seen her Sheena had traveled the world – visiting the capitals of Europe and Asia, the Great Pyramids – and had lived for a time in Abu Dhabi and Atlanta. She returned home to take care of her Mom when she fell ill, and said the garden had given her Mom so much pleasure that she resolved to keep it going after she passed. I imagined that it must take an incredible amount of dedication and effort, and she did it joyfully with the help of a full-time gardener.

She had fully furnished, self-contained flats for rent!! With hot water!! She immediately gave Frank and me a two-bedroom, two-bath flat for the price of a room, to stay in while we were there.

Sheena is also the consummate hostess. In fact, we call her Madam Etiquette or "Mrs. Bucket" from the British TV series "Keeping up Appearances." She has a full-time helper and is always prepared to entertain. Her signature homemade ginger beer is craved by all who've tasted it. It's not unusual for a Member of Parliament or a government official or an executive from a non-profit organization to pop in unannounced. They know they'll be grandly entertained on her verandah that's open to all that beautiful nature. Plus, Sheena has more cousins than she can count, and it's not unusual for people, who come with others to visit, to discover in conversation that they're related.

Soon Frank and I were going to Jamaica every year or two, and I realized that just before I went to sleep at night the image I would conjure up to slip off peacefully was of me lying under the guinep tree. Frank loved it just as much as I did, and he was overjoyed by the profusion and variety of birds and butterflies to watch and photograph and paint, and the variety of fruits he could pick and eat.

It reminded him of growing up in Dania where he said he and his friends would leave home early morning and not come back until dusk, feasting all day on mangoes, oranges, guavas, coconuts, pineapples, sugar apples and avocadoes. Since all of that is long gone now, buried under concrete and condos, he was ecstatic to be able to reprise the experience in Jamaica.

In 2016 when I turned 65 I decided to celebrate with a big party at Sheena's. Cammal and Sheena took the lead, as they're much better at planning than me. Frank and I, Lisa, Monica, Cammal and Carolyn Hartfield flew down for the happy occasion. The night of the party the electricity went out across the entire island. Sheena says that's when she saw what I'm made of, because I was completely unfazed. There was nothing we could do about it, so why get upset? I reasoned that we had candles, we could build a fire outdoors and heat up the food, and it would be an adventure. The lights came on minutes before the party started.

The greatest gift I got that day was to reconnect with my cousin Lillian Canacee Wilmot, Miss Thomas' daughter, with whom I grew up. She's several years younger than me, and we lost touch since I left Summerfield around age 18. I'd always wanted to get in touch with her, but failed until that night. As it turns out, she was looking for me as well, and destiny brought her together with Sheena, her former classmate at the University of the West Indies. Learning that Sheena was a Clarendon College graduate, she asked her if she knew Audrey Wright. Sheena's response, "The birthday party I'm planning is for Audrey Wright" brought us together at last.

As long as we were in Jamaica we wanted to take in some of the sights and the history, so Rhema's younger brother Victor Simpson, who owns a sign printing business, rented a car for us and asked his driver Paul Watson to take us around the island for the weekend. Four rooms on the North Coast for a couple of nights could be pricey, so Sheena called up her friends Hazel and Bobby Binger and they said sure, we could use their villa for the weekend. Perched in the hills above the ocean with a swimming pool and an abundance of fruit trees, all we were required to do was pay the helper who made sumptuous food for us. Such luxury.

Rhema joined us for the weekend and we drove up to Accompong in St. Elizabeth, one of the oldest Maroon communities in the country. The roads were extremely challenging and at one point we actually had to get out of the vehicle so it could navigate the rutted roads. But the welcoming, self-governing community at the end of the drive made it all worth it.

Not long after, Frank and I were in Washington, DC at a birthday party for his friend, Rep. Hastings. I was talking with a lady and mentioned that we'd just got back from Jamaica and went to Accompong.

To my amazement she said, "I'm from Accompong."

Wait, what?

Congresswoman Yvette Clarke is proud of her roots in Accompong, and both she and I were blown away that the subject came up in our conversation. That night we also met the formidable Rep. Maxine Waters and her daughter, as well as Rep. Steny Hoyer, House Majority Leader under Chair Nancy Pelosi.

My birthday weekend continued with a visit to Doctor's Cave Beach in Montego Bay and the Rose Hall Great House. All three destinations are included in the new tour of historical sites being promoted by the Hon. Babsy Grange, Jamaica's Minister of Culture, Gender, Entertainment and Sports. I am so looking forward to visiting them all and soaking up my history and culture, just as I've visited more than 100 of the historic sites in America that are protected in the National Park System.

Sheena remained very involved with Clarendon College, like many of our classmates. Dorrit, Monica and Cammal support the school consistently. I was definitely the low (wo)man on the totem pole. But in 2017 Sheena encouraged the school to invite me to be a guest speaker at the 75th Annual Founders Day celebration. What a privilege!

I told the young people how, exactly 50 years before, I was sitting where they sat. I reminded them of the story of Rev. Davy and the homeless man that past student Hyacinth Broderick captured in her book reprising the school's history. I told them that Rev. Davy already had an education and didn't need to care that others might not have access. But, because of his loving compassionate soul, thousands of us had gotten a high school education, which made all the difference in our lives.

I told them never to be ashamed of where they came from and always to be proud, recounting the modest means I had growing up. Yet I had been invited to meet a U.S. President because of our contributions to society. I encouraged them to provide help wherever they could, to strive to be on time and, if they found they couldn't be punctual, to call and notify whoever was waiting for them. My 10-year-old twin cousins were in the audience because I felt it was important for them to be exposed.

After the celebrations Frank and I were thrilled to visit the Blue and John Crow Mountains National Park. I read an intriguing article about it in Health, Home and Garden Magazine, a fabulous glossy produced by Sheena's friend, Fay Wint, and determined that we couldn't miss the opportunity to visit. I'd been to more than 185 of the 400-plus national park sites in America so I was very excited by the thought of getting to tour this jewel in the land of my birth.

A little research revealed that the park is a World Heritage Site, a UNESCO designation that puts it the same category as the Grand Canyon, Yellowstone, Yosemite and others - part of the heritage of all mankind. Wow!

Ms. Wint connected us with Symerna Blake from the park's marketing office, and she set up a tour for us that began with transportation up to the park in the comfortable vehicle provided by Kool Tours and driven by Mr. Gary Hooper. It took about an hour from Devon House in Kingston where he picked us up, and our eyes and hearts were filled with the beauty of the mountains spreading out all around us.

Ms. Blake arranged for us to stay at the lovely Heritage House at Cold Springs, a very comfortable and well-appointed lodging in which we were the only guests for the night. The caretakers made a point of telling us that as they left for the evening, and told us that they'd be in the very back of the property if we needed them. Sitting out on the verandah with a drink at dusk, secluded from the road and watching the lights come on around Kingston Harbor at dusk – well, just wow!

We went to the park's Visitor Center in Holywell and talked with the park rangers, and our spirits were filled by the beauty all around, the vast knowledge base of the rangers, and the joy of being educated by our Black countrymen and women. Next morning we woke up very early and went on a birding tour with a ranger who took us to the spots where he knew we would see some of the most exciting avian denizens of the forest. When we saw Spot-breasted Orioles and Striped-faced Tanagers zooming through the tall trees, spotted the secretive Mountain Witch bobbing her way up the road, and spied a tiny Tody – with an emerald green body and bright red throat - grooming itself in a tree, we felt as if we really were in Heaven without having to die. I can hardly wait to go back.

I make an effort to be happy wherever I am and not to pine for other circumstances. So when I found myself yearning more and more to be at Sheena's, I kept saying to her,

"Why can't I come and live here?"

Laughing, she replied, "You can. I have furnished flats for rent."

She thought I was joking, and I was kind of joking, but suddenly the thought made complete sense.

And when Frank said, "What do you want to do?" I could see it clearly.

"How about we go and take a flat at Sheena's for a while?"

"I can live with that," he said.

****

CHAPTER TWENTY-SIX

We got Limitless ready and put her on the market, turning her over to the same broker who'd sold her to us. Then we spent some time cleaning out our storage, giving away things we hadn't used in years, and packing up our books and all the paintings and sculptures Frank had done, to ship to Jamaica.

We'd stayed with our friends Lee and Jimmy for nine months while the boat was refurbished in 2011 and, once we put the boat on the market, we were able to stay with them until we left for Jamaica.

I was looking forward to spending time with my Auntie B who still lived with her grandchildren at the house where I was born, talking about the old days and learning some new things from her. Our tentative date to arrive in Jamaica was November 15, 2018.

Mid-October my cousin Marsha called and told me Auntie B was sick. It didn't sound like anything dreadfully serious, but within a few days she was dead.

I regretted that I would not be able to sit down by the gully and reminisce with her but I didn't grieve because I reason that, if death is inevitable, then it's the quality of life that the person lived and the good they did that matters.

Still, it was hard to avoid the sadness. We arrived November 7, just three days before the funeral. We went up to the old house to see the family and found her children distraught at the suddenness of her passing. I was concerned about how her death might affect her young grandsons.

Auntie B's brother, one of Mass D's children from his second marriage, preached at the funeral. I learned how diligently my aunt served God and that she regularly walked to different people's homes in the neighborhood that she said God told her needed prayer. She was also an usher at her church, much loved and very highly regarded.

I was really surprised to hear a reference to obeah and an exhortation from one of her sons for people to stop practicing obeah. I was even more shocked later when I asked what that reference was about. The twins told me with great seriousness that someone had sent obeah to someone else in the village and it accidentally caught Auntie B.

Say what?! I mean, Frank calls me an obeah woman but I didn't know that it was still a real thing in Jamaican life. I told the boys I don't believe there's any such thing, and that whatever you believe is what will manifest in your life. I don't know if it changed their minds and I'm not concerned. I don't see it as my place to convince them what to believe. I share what I know in case it might be helpful to them, and then I let it go.

The beauties of living at Sheena's are compounded every day. First off, she suggested we take a flat that was completely detached and looks right out onto her lavish garden. A huge Number 11 mango tree is outside our front door and in season mangoes land on our roof in the middle of the night with a whopping thud. The first few nights it was a little startling, but waking up in the morning and finding multiple succulent mangoes a few steps away more than make up for it. We got used to the sound in no time.

Right outside my kitchen window is a big guava tree which so far has only produced a few guavas so I watch eagerly for every sign of one. Directly behind it is a fence draped in verdant bougainvillea blooms of orange, red, and purple that I can also see from our bed. Beyond that is an open field with several large trees and in the distance I can see a few rooftops. Much farther away I can see the mountains that ring Clarendon like the sides of a bowl.

Red bougainvillea grow all the way up to our bedroom window as if peeping inside. Behind them is a small garden of perennially blooming red ginger and yellow lobster claws.

Out the guest bathroom window a big sweetsop tree is a favorite stop of a male Jamaican Doctor Bird. I can be brushing my teeth and spying on a banana quit grooming itself a few feet away.

The flat is designed to let the outside in so I always feel as if I'm outdoors. Sitting on my couch or out on my veranda, I see through the French doors the garden spreading out in front of me 500 yards down to the gate. I can see traffic passing by and the occasional person. Goats and dogs roam freely across the road outside.

In the mornings I wake up to the sound of roosters crowing and the neighbors' gorgeous red and white roosters strut their way past the kitchen window followed by pretty varicolored hens. They peck at the food peelings we throw under the guava tree and scratch under the cherry tree.

I notice that food spoils here much faster than in the States and we are happy about that, as it signals that they're fresh and probably lacking preservatives.

Maybe the best part of all is that Sheena and I can talk from our verandas. Imagine that you have a friend from your earliest days in high school that you wind up living with in your late 60s. We have so many things in common and so many points of reference, we are laughing and joking all the time. I am continuously amazed that she can call my name and I can hear her from my flat, and I can do the same thing. Most often she's calling to give us something - guineps that her gardener just picked; Otaheite apples that her friend down the road just brought up; calaloo and pak choy that a farmer brought her, or a couple of hot patties that she brought us back from her trip to May Pen.

As the volunteer Emergency Chair of the Jamaica Red Cross Clarendon Branch, and an officer of the May Pen Chamber of Commerce and Industry, she's very involved in the community. A supporter of innumerable people and causes, she enjoys a very special place in the parish and local life. It all inures to our benefit because she gives us the option of being involved or not.

We don't have a car as I don't plan to drive in Jamaica – we drive on the opposite side of the road from America where I drove for 40 years. Besides, in many places the roads are deeply rutted and you really need to know what you're doing in order to navigate them. So when she's going into town she invites me and we go to the market and stores together.

Sheena has more cousins than I could ever imagine one person having. Recently two sisters from England accompanied a friend visiting her, and in conversation discovered they were her cousins. At Christmas she took us with her to multiple cousins' lavish celebrations in beautiful Bog Walk, their estate on a hill overlooking endless vistas of rolling mountains covered in greenery, dotted with Flame of the Forest trees shocking out in orange blooms. On Christmas Day we went to another cousin's dinner party where the family actually has a full-time chef. Everyone embraces us like part of the family.

Driving down the street from her house Sheena points out her cousins' homes, and it's practically every other house! The Boulevard was named for her family that's been in the area for more than 100 years. You can't get much more grounded than that.

My kitchen and living room windows face east, so in the mornings I see the first fingers of pink or yellow probe their way above the green mountains. It is a joy beyond compare to watch the sun rise and pay homage to it, proof of Earth's continued revolution on its axis as it travels around the sun. Wow!

I picture the Earth turning different sides of its face to the sun to create morning on our side while causing nightfall in England. I have driven across the breadth of the United States so I know the landscape that will see the sun at different times until the Pacific side gets it three hours later than the Eastern Seaboard. I visualize the Earth pulling the moon behind it in its orbit as it travels 365 days around the sun, creating a calendar year.

Wow!! How can anyone on Earth possibly say they're bored when we live in such a dynamic universe? In these moments I feel closest to God. The sense of gratitude persists all day as I consciously make myself remember who and what I am, a child of God intimately and inseparably connected to that life-force.

I feel a deep connection with the higglers in May Pen Market who remind me of my Grandma Ida as they sell fresh foodstuffs and fruit. I'm told you're supposed to bargain with them so that they lower the price, but having the experience of how Mama's earnings provided for us, I'm happy to pay whatever they ask and consider it money well spent. Oh, the perfect avocados and papayas and Millie mangoes and June plum and – endless varieties of fresh ripe fruit and green vegetables.

Once I heard a young lady ask a woman selling watermelon if it was sweet, and if she would cut a piece so she could taste it. I could hardly believe my eyes when the seller obliged and, pronouncing it good, the young lady bought half. I quickly bought the other half. I cannot imagine that happening in the U.S.

In the ValuMart Supermarket where I shop at I often see the staff looking at me admiringly.

"Excuse me, miss. Are you a teacher?"

"No, but I play one on TV." (Just kidding, I don't actually say that.)

A young man named Paul tells me he looks out for me and happily helps me do my shopping and carries my cloth bags to the corner. The Jamaican government banned plastic bags on January 1, 2019 and I haven't heard one person complain. Everyone seems happy to do their part to "protect our environment."

At the corner several young men have pushcarts from which they sell ripe papaya, watermelon, pineapples and many varieties of fruit. They slice the fruit into small portions and put them in sandwich bags so people don't have to buy a large quantity. They always call out to me and, if I haven't already been to the market, they peel and slice my sugar pine, cut me some watermelon and pick out a nice firm papaya for me. Then they go and try to get me a taxi.

The taxis have designated routes inked onto the driver's door, and sometimes it's hard to see the route before the vehicle passes you. I love to stand there in the middle of town with the crowds undulating around me and reggae music pounding from the cart of the guy selling CDs outside. It's not unusual to see people bust a little move because the rhythm is so compelling. In the few months since I've been home, the taxi drivers on my route have gotten to know me and now they stop for me before I even recognize them. Taxis are the major means of transportation and usually have multiple passengers. Now I have the contact information for several drivers who will come and pick us up and take us wherever we want to go, and wait for us if we want them to.

I used to tell Frank how odd I found it having to call friends before I visit them in America when I first migrated. In the early days after returning home to Jamaica, I used to wonder why Rhema or Tom who live just about 10 minutes away, or Earl or other friends don't call before they come over, and I burst out laughing when I realized the irony.

On Wednesdays Sheena's full-time helper Juliet Thomas comes to work for us, washing, cleaning and best of all, cooking the most delectable dishes and stacking them in the fridge for the week.

I've had a very vibrant community of friends on Facebook for at least a decade, connected mostly through environmental, climate and political issues. Then by some great stroke of fortune, late 2018

I lucked upon the group Vintage Jamaica, which serves Jamaicans in the diaspora. Many of the members live overseas.

I started sharing the experiences I'm enjoying after 40 years away and really struck a chord. People are so eager to revisit the shared memories of our youth, but many are reluctant to return home because of the fear of violence that is much highlighted overseas. They're also concerned that they may not be able to access the same level of health care as they can in North America and Britain. I point out that, while there is crime in Jamaica as unfortunately there is crime almost everywhere, the majority of Jamaicans live very enjoyable and contented lives.

This group was the single biggest inducement for me to write this book, as they continually encouraged me. I felt impelled to salute some of the most consistent supporters in my acknowledgements.

Around this time Sheena got a new puppy that she named Prince, and we became devoted to each other. I'd have to write another book to convey how much it helped me to have this little darling requiring me to take breaks to go out and play with him as we chased each other around the garden. When I go out at sunrise he follows me and while I'm praying facing the sun he happily snuffles through the undergrowth nearby.

To go back to where I began this story, on Sunday August 25 Rhema, Earl and Tom picked up Frank and me and took us down to Rocky Point which was like going on a mini vacation. The beach is mostly eroded and tires have been placed along the water's edge to try and reduce the effect. The festive atmosphere in town, the incredibly fresh snapper fish starting at one pound, steamed with crackers and okra or fried and served with bammy, can only be described as finger-licking good. Once again I was a child happily gorging myself with not a care in the world. Then Earl picked up the tab. What a great day!

Looked at one way, I fled political turmoil and violence in Jamaica in 1978, and exactly 40 years later I reverse migrated for pretty much the same reason – political turmoil in the US.

We were at Sheena's Election Night 2016 and deliberately turned off all our devices. The morning after, I saw Miss Shirley, the housekeeper for Sheena's another tenant, pushing her bicycle up the driveway.

"Do you know who won the elections, Miss Shirley?" I called out.

"Trunk, ma'm. Trunk won," she called back.

"What?" I asked, planet reeling.

"Yes ma'm. Trunk won!"

I had written prolifically before the elections about what a Trump win would mean for the environment. Now I am happier than ever that we decided to put some distance between us and the constant rancor, though we can watch CNN all day if we choose.

As someone who has imbibed the history of America, from the places where it happened and who knows what our ancestors Black, White, red and yellow invested in building the country, I feel compelled to continue to play my part. I do it with my pen – figuratively – by posting consistently on social media, reminding Americans of the legacy we have to live up to and the legacy we are creating.

I publish a blog at least once every month looking at current events through the prism of the eternal national parks and forests, and Frank and I return periodically to the U.S. for speaking engagements. That's how we were able to wade into the water August 1, 2019 at the spot where our African ancestors came ashore August 25, 1619. Thankfully our perspective is still regularly sought in interviews and we're happy to contribute. We also continue managing the Diverse Environmental Leaders Speakers Bureau. From Florida to Tasmania, members are spreading the message of inclusion and the urgency of addressing the climate crisis. If everyone does all he or she can, it must be enough.

CHAPTER TWENTY-SEVEN

Saturday, October 11 2019, my cousin Canacee picked us up for the trip up to the country to visit my birthplace and her mom Miss Thomas who kept baby Lisa when my Grandma Ida went into the hospital. Though we communicate through WhatsApp we hadn't spent much time with each other, so the ride through the May Pen woods, up to Chapelton and down Trafalgar Hill plumbed depths of time and space – not only the hour that it took us, but 60 years of memory.

I showed her and Frank the place in the May Pen woods where our friends finally came and picked up Sheena and me at the back of the pack on a sponsored 13-mile walk to raise funds for our school. In Chapelton the bakery where we used to buy bulla and Cush bread after school is still standing. I pointed out where the library used to be that I used to haunt for the latest Nancy Drew or Bobbsey Twins books, and the gates of my school, made famous by the exploits of so many students past and present, the latest being as winners of the DaCosta Cup in 2019.

Trafalgar Hill, which I recall being dauntingly steep, appears now as a mere slope, and the Otaheite apple tree we used to climb is still standing near the bottom of the hill. The major difference is that the Danks orange groves – acres and acres of oranges that we used to treat as if it belonged to all of us children – is now overgrown and the oranges gone. There's a big new sign announcing that we're entering Summer Field at the same point where the road diverges and there's a sign pointing to Dorrit's community, Mullet Hall.

The bridge over the St. Thomas River is still there and I point out the place where the lone movie theater used to be. I tell them how moviegoers would shout out to the actors on screen, "Him back a you!!" "See him a come deh!" and in the case of the crucifixion movie, "Lawd, no beat the ooman pickney so!! Him a summady pickney, you know!"

Things don't appear to have changed much in the little town and the buildings could definitely use refurbishing and a new coat of paint. I point out where Mr. Nash's shop used to be where Mama bought the material for my school clothes. I used to love going there and looking at all the pretty fabric. Further up the road is the Chins' shop, and the town is just starting to come alive with clothing vendors setting up their wares outside the stores. I expected the bustling market scene that used to be there on Saturdays when Mama went to market and took me with her, higglers congregated along the roadside selling foodstuffs, mostly ground produce – yam and banana, potatoes, dashene and coco, dug fresh from the ground.

Most times Mama left me at home to clean the house, which mainly consisted of washing and polishing the floor using a coconut brush and red Rexo polish. The coconut brush was made by cutting off some of the husk at the end of a dried coconut and leaving bristles that could really put a shine on the dyed floor. We polished the floor on our hands and knees. You could tell who was polishing the floor at their house by the dark spots on their knees. I learned early on to put a rag under my knees to protect them.

We drove into the village past the little house where Mama lived her last few years, past the Leibas' big house on the hill, past my cousin Blanche's house - she's long gone - past brother Cecil and Miss Mulvena's house which looks deserted, and past their shop which is now occupied by a tailor. We passed the place where the big cotton tree used to be, that all the children would run fast to pass at night, as everybody knows that duppy live under cotton tree. Reaching the turnoff to her Mom's, Canacee said we'd continue up to my birth home and give her mom a little more time to get ready for visitors.

We passed our old Church of God which is now a huge building, and I showed them where the standpipe used to be, next to a grove of bamboo trees that the wind would set singing and creaking. They're gone now. We passed Annie and Olive Williams' house, past Zoe's house and Audrey Bloomfield's house, passed the other cotton tree still standing and almost passed my house. We drove across the old stone bridge and heard my gully rushing with water and saw it flowing over a drop on the side. How wonderful. We had to drive a bit to find a place to turn around.

My birth home is showing its age and part of the verandah has fallen down. It's clear it's no longer habitable and I am so glad that Auntie B was able to get a pre-fabricated government house and set it down where the kitchen used to be. I gather that her older grandson in his 20s, a welder who used to live with her, is still living there. I can hear the TV on in the house but no one responds to our call.

Oh, dear God! Walking into the yard I'm in a daze, sure-footed on the slippery sloping path down to the gully. My gully is still there!! And better than ever!! Last time I saw it at Auntie B's funeral a year earlier it was choked with weeds, but now the weeds are all gone and the gully is flowing joyful and free. It's gurgling with joy to see me, as I am screaming with joy to see it.

I put my toes in and the cool water takes me back, so far back. I wade in and look up to see the common mango tree still there, looking strong as ever. The gully banks on that side are thick with greenery and a tree has conveniently fallen across the gully, allowing me to step up and survey the whole area from a lofty perch.

I wonder if Mama is here with me, if Mass D is here, if every thought and action that ever took place in this space is held forever in the ether somewhere. I am enfolded, and I am free. I wonder how they'd feel now if they could see me and talk with me. I bet they'd say. "I knew you would turn into something." Like Bob Marley sang, I'm happy and sad at the same time.

Leaving my gully we drive a few chains farther down and I could have jumped out of my skin when I saw my breadfruit tree. What a big, beautiful vibrant tree! And it's still bearing, one lonely breadfruit sitting near the top. I was so excited to pick my way down to the river and hug the tree, I didn't even notice the breadfruit that Canacee mentioned.

The roots of the breadfruit tree are almost down in the gully, so it has a constant supply of water. A cocoa tree is growing underneath, its roots intertwined and also drinking from the gully. Big ripe yellow cocoa pods remind me of the seeds inside covered with a sticky sweetness. As a child we'd break the hard shell, suck off the gooey seeds then wash them in the gully and put them out to dry. Then we'd parch and roast them and beat them in a mortar, creating a supple, slightly oily paste that we'd mold into chocolate in the shape of a gig, or spinning top. The dried chocolates could last indefinitely until we were ready to grate and place it in boiling water to make a rich chocolate tea.

But, my breadfruit tree and my gully, together! Of all the joys I've experienced in my life for which I am so grateful, this ranks high among them. Just like that I was transported back to my earliest origins – my umbilical cord that connected me to my mother, and her mother, and innumerable generations of mothers that led to me, is in this place, part of this tree. I conceive of it as a symbiotic relationship, the stem cells in my navel string - which are now widely preserved to aid in repelling disease - helped nurture this tree and the tree in turn nurturing many members of my family. Its roots hold and stabilize the embankment above the river which is susceptible to landslides.

As I'm giving thanks down below, Canace calls me from the road telling me that Miss Icy has come down from her house and I should come up now if I want to see her. Well of course I want to see anyone from the old days. I'm not sure I remember her but she says she remembers me. We hug, and I press a few dollars into her hands. She's on her way to clean up the church and we talk about what a devoted servant of God my Auntie B was.

Next comes Mass Lando Dunkley from his field, carrying his machete. We recollect how he and I were baptized the same day by Brother Foster in Big River and laugh about how long ago that was. I last saw him at Auntie B's funeral and he reminded me I'd said I would come back to visit. "I'm here now," I laugh.

Then we progress to Miss Thomas house, where I am shocked to find an elegant upstairs residence and two smaller houses in the compound. We walk past two cheerful yellow cottages and up the ramp into Miss Thomas' beautiful, well-ordered home with the spacious rooms leading to her balcony.

There she rose up to greet us, so beautiful and smiling, her hair fully white - ohh! I was so happy as we hugged. I wanted to see her for so long, and here she was at 88 looking better and more vital than I could ever have expected.

Sitting on the verandah facing the green scalloped mountains in the distance; seeing shiny red ackees in the yard; ripe key limes on the tree; blades of cane where the path used to cross over from my house, I got a feeling I might be able to describe if I was a better writer. It was like coming home, going backward and going forward simultaneously. All the old people were there. That was Sister Sam's house in yellow right there. Brother Sam's land below the road is sporting multiple tin roofs where the land has been "captured" and people have built houses. To get to the gully bank where I used to sit I will need to ask them for permission to pass through their yard. I'm leaving that for the future.

Miss Thomas corroborates everything I remember and adds one vital fact – when Mama fled from Mass D, we came to live with her and Brother Reggie for a while before we moved over to Uncle Baugh. That house is gone now and the land is covered in small trees. She and Canacee and I reminisce about the cashew tree and the parching parties; the tumultuous years of Ding Dong who has gone to live with his daughter in May Pen and his pet peeve is, Why do preachers have to shout so much, do they think Jesus is deaf?

Miss Thomas' helper is a sprightly lady in her 70s and has prepared meals for the weekend before leaving at noon to go shopping in May Pen. Canacee opens some coconuts that have already been cut and we drink coconut water and eat jelly, followed by escoveitched fish with hardough bread. Morning passes into afternoon and we're just sitting there comfortably walking down memory lane and watching the shadows move across the mountains as the clouds change position.

When we finally say our goodbyes, it is so great to know that I have a place to come back and stay for a night or two if I like, because this is deep country and there are no hotels or Airbnb's. We have all the conveniences of home – running water, flush toilet, electricity and gas stove and that most precious thing to me, a place to sit and look at the view. Best of all, I can sleep within walking distance of my breadfruit tree, my birth home and my cousins.

When we got home that evening Frank said, "Honey, you are glowing. You look so vital and dynamic."

Well of course I think I look like that all the time, but I am glad it showed externally.

I can go back home again! I am so grateful.

****

EPILOGUE

I'm just learning about Jamaica's environmental situation and pleased to observe that the general public appears very positively disposed to protect what we have. A major controversy surrounds the government's proposal to mine areas of our pristine Cockpit Country. A distinction is being made between a "protected area" and an unprotected area, and citizens are lined up on either side. Many residents in the area where mining is proposed believe it will provide jobs and improve their economic situation. Others are adamantly opposed to a breach and the permanent effect it will have on the area and its resources, including farming and wildlife.

From my experience in the U.S., industries that woo people with the promise of jobs seldom deliver, bringing in their own employees to hold the better-paying positions. Researching the situation for this book, I found an article written by the erudite Gleaner columnist Michael Witter. He cited how one of the leaders opposing the bauxite development asked "why we should sabotage their way of life for, at most, 30 more years of bauxite production with marginal gains to the country, almost none of which would reach the people of the yam belt."

Mr. Witter recalled the words of a ganja farmer he interviewed in the Great Morass Swamp in St. Elizabeth 40 years earlier when the government at that time proposed to mine for peat in the swamp to fuel a power plant for perhaps 30 years.

"He looked at me quizzically and said, 'Needless yu sell u brekfus fi buy yu dinna.'"

Mr. Witter wrote that because the swamp had not been breached, today it is thriving and now there's "the possibility of accessing a rapidly growing global market" for marijuana.

There could hardly be a better example of why we must not sacrifice long-term sustainability for short-term gains.

I've also been fortunate to connect with Ms. Ingrid Parchment, Executive Director of the Caribbean Coastal Area Management Foundation. A longtime friend of Sheena's, she's promised to take us down to the conservation area so I can literally "get my feet wet" and develop an appreciation for what is going on. I want to be of service to my country as I have been to the U.S.

So I guess Mom was right. All I needed was my shoes and my handbag, the knowledge and information, because I definitely had the passion.

Over the years my heels were often an item of conversation – I had women friends from the opposite end of the socio-economic spectrum that looked forward to comparing our shoes at Board meetings. Once when we were touring Theodore Roosevelt's birth home in New York City my friend and I were admiring each other's fashionable high heels, and the group went on ahead of us. We didn't know where they were, and we opened a door and stepped through just as the ranger was walking into the room and telling the group, "and this is the secret door...." Everyone burst into laughter at the look on our faces, like children caught in the act.

When we lived on Limitless, even the Secretary of the Interior with whom I'd served nine years on a Board asked me, "WHERE do you store all your shoes on a boat?!"

I don't have the same attachment to handbags though.

Now Sheena tells us she's noticing more about the wildlife on her property since we came.

"I'm watching the woodpeckers and the Pechary and the Banana Quit that I barely noticed before. You are what you were," she says sagely, referring to my love for nature and my early communication skills.

True. I still feel like that little girl who sat on the banks of the gully all those years ago. With so much more experience and wisdom, but the same sense of absolute wonder and joy.

Thank You, God!

****

ABOUT THE AUTHOR

AUDREY WRIGHT: Debating Society, 4-H, Drama, Editor. Her only claim to fame is her mellifluous voice which makes even the rubbish she spurts sound like sense. Beware!

Despite the admonition from her high school classmates to "beware" the mellifluent voice of Audrey Wright, she grew up to become a sought-after, award winning speaker across the United States. Mrs. Peterman is recognized as a leader in the effort to make the environmental field more inclusive. With her husband Frank, she is co-author of *Legacy on the Land: A Black Couple Discovers Our National Inheritance and Tells Why Every American Should Care*, 2009. She is the author of *Our True Nature: Finding A Zest for Life in the National Park System*, 2012. The mother of a blended family of six, she has 19 grandchildren and five great-grandchildren. Mrs. Peterman and her husband reside in Jamaica and the United States.